*'These poems are the answers to every question you ever wanted to ask, and the question for every answer you wanted to question. Funny, informative and intriguing, this book will expand your brain to twice its size.'*
**MICHAEL ROSEN**

For Jake, George and Evie, who have always asked such interesting questions, love Dad xx – B.B.

For Tils, Beabo and Marth, with huge love, Papa xxx – J.B.

First published in Great Britain in 2025 by Red Shed, part of Farshore
An imprint of HarperCollins*Publishers*
1 London Bridge Street, London SE1 9GF
www.farshore.co.uk

HarperCollins*Publishers*
Macken House, 39/40 Mayor Street Upper
Dublin 1, D01 C9W8, Ireland

Red Shed is a registered trademark of HarperCollins*Publishers* Ltd.

Text © Brian Bilston 2025
Illustrations © Joe Berger 2025
Brian Bilston and Joe Berger have asserted their moral rights.

978 0 00 868280 4
Printed in Bosnia and Herzegovina
002

A CIP catalogue record for this title is available from the British Library.

All rights reserved. No part of this publication may be reproduced, stored in a retrieval system, or transmitted, in any form or by any means, electronic, mechanical, photocopying, recording or otherwise, without the prior permission of the publisher and copyright owner.

Without limiting the author's and publisher's exclusive rights, any unauthorised use of this publication to train generative artificial intelligence (AI) technologies is expressly prohibited. HarperCollins also exercise their rights under Article 4(3) of the Digital Single Market Directive 2019/790 and expressly reserve this publication from the text and data mining exception.

Stay safe online. Any website addresses listed in this book are correct at the time of going to print. However, Farshore is not responsible for content hosted by third parties. Please be aware that online content can be subject to change and websites can contain content that is unsuitable for children. We advise that all children are supervised when using the internet.

This book contains FSC™ certified paper and other controlled sources to ensure responsible forest management.

For more information visit: www.harpercollins.co.uk/green

BRIAN BILSTON

JOE BERGER

# A POEM FOR EVERY QUESTION

RED SHED

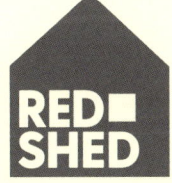

# CONTENTS

| | |
|---|---|
| How many different bugs are there in your house? | 10 |
| When did Tyrannosaurus live? | 12 |
| What causes a tornado? | 13 |
| Can fire cast a shadow? | 14 |
| Can poo heat your home? | 16 |
| How many stars in the Universe exploded today? | 17 |
| Who had the first holiday? | 18 |
| What was the biggest gift ever? | 20 |
| Why does an onion have layers? | 21 |
| How many times a day do we laugh? | 22 |
| Which is the biggest country in the world? | 24 |
| Are the Egyptian pyramids the only pyramids? | 25 |
| How much rubbish is there around Earth in space? | 26 |
| How many bones does a baby have? | 27 |
| What are nightmares? | 28 |
| Why do my fingers and toes wrinkle in water? | 30 |
| Why don't trees burst in winter like cold pipes? | 31 |
| Which is the biggest animal? | 32 |
| How do clouds work? | 34 |
| Why do we fart? | 35 |
| What were the seven wonders of the ancient world? | 36 |
| Are unicorns real? | 38 |
| When was the internet born? | 40 |
| How deep is Earth's crust? | 41 |
| Which animals have more than one brain? | 42 |

| | |
|---|---|
| What is the largest single living organism on Earth? | 43 |
| What does gravity do? | 44 |
| Why can't I roll my tongue? | 44 |
| What is the world's oldest instrument? | 45 |
| Who carved the faces of four US presidents in a mountain? | 46 |
| Which bird's wings beat the fastest? | 47 |
| Will a great white shark eat me? | 48 |
| How far away is Mars? | 50 |
| Why do people hug? | 52 |
| Can you see the Great Wall of China from space? | 53 |
| How did the ancient Egyptians make a mummy? | 54 |
| If a coin fell from the Empire State Building, would it kill you? | 56 |
| Could a woman be a gladiator? | 58 |
| How do planes fly upside down? | 59 |
| How many teeth does a crocodile have? | 60 |
| Where is the hottest place on Earth? | 62 |
| What is a primary colour? | 64 |
| Why does thunder rumble? | 66 |
| How did Beethoven compose music when he was deaf? | 67 |
| How many astronauts have gone to the Moon? | 68 |
| Is zillion a real number? | 69 |
| Why does milk go bad? | 70 |
| Is there a monster in Loch Ness? | 71 |
| What's inside a tennis ball? | 72 |
| Did dinosaurs have feathers? | 74 |
| Why does my heart beat? | 76 |

| | |
|---|---|
| Where is the deepest place in Earth's oceans? | 77 |
| What is the difference between an emigrant and an immigrant? | 78 |
| How does a honeybee build its hive? | 80 |
| Why do things float? | 81 |
| How far away is the Sun? | 82 |
| What is a black hole? | 83 |
| How long can you survive in a desert if you drank your own pee? | 84 |
| What is a right angle? | 85 |
| Who invented football? | 86 |
| When were the first Olympics? | 88 |
| What are rainbows made of? | 89 |
| Why does a lion have a mane? | 90 |
| Why do clouds float? | 92 |
| How do animals survive in freezing seas? | 93 |
| Are bats the only flying mammals? | 94 |
| Do elephants really hold each other's tails? | 96 |
| Which country first used paper money? | 97 |
| How young can the US President be? | 98 |
| Which sport was played on the Moon? | 100 |
| Why do we get bruises? | 101 |
| Why does the Leaning Tower of Pisa lean? | 102 |
| Why should we recycle? | 103 |
| Are Olympic gold medals made of real gold? | 104 |
| What was the first animal to be cloned? | 105 |
| Who invented the first car? | 106 |
| Who made the first trip around the world? | 107 |

| | |
|---|---|
| Why do animals migrate? | 108 |
| Why do I need to eat a lot of fruit and vegetables? | 110 |
| What wood is a cricket bat made of? | 111 |
| Which animal hides the best? | 112 |
| What is the difference between a stalactite and a stalagmite? | 114 |
| What are animals without a backbone called? | 116 |
| What is a dimension? | 117 |
| Was Blackbeard a real pirate? | 118 |
| Do cats always land on their feet? | 119 |
| Are horses even or odd-toed? | 120 |
| Are coal and diamonds the same thing? | 121 |
| What is the jet stream? | 122 |
| What is absolute zero? | 123 |
| Can it rain fish? | 124 |
| How long is the marathon? | 125 |
| How did people make the first tools if they did not have tools? | 126 |
| Why do some animals have pouches? | 127 |
| Which country has the most bicycles? | 128 |
| How many dimples are there on a golf ball? | 130 |
| Which mountain is the highest in the world? | 131 |
| Which river is the longest? | 132 |
| Can you say the alphabet in code? | 134 |
| Who is the champion weightlifter of the animal world? | 136 |
| Glossary | 138 |
| About the author and illustrator | 141 |

## HOW MANY DIFFERENT BUGS ARE THERE IN YOUR HOUSE?

Or more to the point,
as we were discussing at last month's Bug Club Meeting
in the downstairs loo,
how many humans are there in our house?

Nigel, one of the woodworms
who's been busy munching his way through the desk
in the first-floor back bedroom,
claims he's spotted three of the things,

whereas Chloe, the carpet beetle
who lives under the sofa in the sitting room,
reckons there's at least seven.
Craig, the fruit fly, disputes that; he says there are four,

but then again, he's only been here for a few days,
and seems to spend most of his time
flitting around that bunch of mouldy bananas
in the fruit bowl on the counter.

Daphne the flea, on the other antenna,
calculates there may be as many as twenty of them;
she's been hanging out with the cat for the last few weeks
and has been all over the house,

# WHEN DID TYRANNOSAURUS LIVE?

What's that? You think the *Jurassic*?
Nah, mate, that's a classic
mistake, that is, because of the movie.

No, scientists have proved he
was actually from the Cretaceous.

*But when exactly?* Goodness gracious!
Well, if you really want to know,
between seventy and sixty-six million years ago,

although I feel I should level with you:
that might be out by an hour or two.

Yes, Tyrannosaurus lived in the Cretaceous period, although it often gets mistaken for belonging to the Jurassic period, thanks to the appearance of Rexy in the film *Jurassic Park*. With its 1.2 metre-long jaws and 30 centimetre-long teeth, Tyrannosaurus was the top predator in town. It's estimated that about 20,000 of them roamed Earth at any one time, and they lived in what is now western USA. There was a lot going on in the Cretaceous: there were more dinosaurs than ever before, insects and flowering plants were everywhere, new types of mammals came on the scene, and the first birds appeared.

## WHAT CAUSES A TORNADO?

So then, where best should I begin
to tell you how **TORNADOES** spin?
One starts, I guess, with a thunderstorm –
a supercell – in which a vortex forms,
a **whizzing**, **whirling**, **swirling** tunnel,
that siphons warm air like a funnel,
**UP** and out, with cold air **DOWN**,
until the vortex tilts; it **SPINS** around,
an ever-faster spiralled cloud,
**stretching** out, down to the ground,
and sets off on its deadly course,
a wild, unstoppable,
untamed
force.

I hope that gives you the basic gist.
They tend to get you in a twist
and so one more thing before we're done . . .
should you see one, you'd better run.

Tornadoes start from violent thunderstorms, known as 'supercells'. Inside these supercells, a whirling funnel of air is created with high-level winds pushing it from behind and surface winds from in front. The vortex (a funnel of air) lifts upright and pulls away from the supercell to become a tornado that can leave behind a trail of devastation. Tornadoes happen all over the world, but the USA has the most: more than 1,000 a year. The wildest ones have wind speeds of more than 480 kilometres per hour.

## CAN FIRE CAST A SHADOW?

*Or rather, how Fire lost its shadow . . .*

Once upon a very long time ago, Fire and Shadow were inseparable, the very best of friends.

Whenever Fire would awaken from her bed of sticks and twigs, her red and orange flames flickering into life to dance merrily in the air, Shadow would copy her movements shyly in the darkness.

'How magically you dance!' Fire would say as she whirled with her friend to the crackle and hiss. 'That is because I have such a wonderful teacher,' Shadow would blush in reply, as light and dark locked in warm embrace.

But one day, when Fire was blazing more intensely than usual, she looked at her friend to see her only half there. 'Shadow!' Fire exclaimed in alarm, 'Whatever has become of you? You are disappearing before my eyes!'

And Shadow replied, 'It is your flames, my faithful, fiery friend. They are too hot for me. I am slowly melting in their heat.'

At this, Fire began to cry but her tears were not enough to stop the flames from growing even larger, and she watched on helplessly as poor Shadow shrank, then disappeared from sight.

Overcome with grief and anger, Fire rampaged across the countryside for seven days and seven nights, until her rage wore itself out and she could burn no more.

And from that day forward, whenever Fire is stirred from her slumbers, she no longer dances the merry dance of old, but her flames sway sadly in the air around her, or flicker with anger at the loss of her friend.

And that is the story of how Fire lost its Shadow . . .

except for the other story that is, the one put about by scientists, which says that Fire never had Shadow in the first place – because Shadow is formed only when light is blocked. And Fire, being a source of light itself, cannot do this.

But, you know, whatever.

The scientists are right: fire cannot typically cast a shadow. Shadows are formed when an object blocks light; the flames of a fire, though, are not solid enough to do that and light is able to pass through. So we must thank science for shedding light on the matter, although that shouldn't stop us from loving some of the old stories either, whether or not they happen to be true.

## CAN POO HEAT YOUR HOME?

*Ten Campaign Headlines Commissioned by the Poo Marketing Board*

1. Help to put the planet straight –
   To heat your home, just defecate!

2. It's the energy source you can renew.
   There's nothing like a number two!

3. It's reusable. It's excellent.
   Power your house with excrement.

4. Want the fossil fuels to stop?
   The answer's in you. The answer's plop.

5. To save the Earth we must make haste –
   Don't let your waste go to waste.

6. 'Because we're worth it' is our refrain.
   It's methane-rich. It's worth the strain.

7. Want to light a room? Or heat your soup?
   All you need's a little poop.

8. It's a beautiful world. Let's not spoil it.
   Harness the power of the toilet.

9. It's the wonder that never ceases –
   Fabulous, fertile, fuel-filled faeces!

10. Make the change. Don't be dumb.
    Use what comes out yer bum.

Poo absolutely can be used for heating and scientists are working on ever better ways to process and use it. A renewable, methane-rich source of energy called 'biogas' can be produced from poo. This can be used as a natural gas, to supply homes and businesses with heat and energy for cooking; to power engines and machines; and to run vehicles as an alternative to petrol and diesel. So come on, everyone, shout it loud and shout it proud . . . POWER TO THE POO-PLE!

# HOW MANY STARS IN THE UNIVERSE EXPLODED TODAY?

Dear Sun,

We thought we would write you this ode
to ask if you'd kindly please not explode,
because eight thousand stars blew up today –
we're glad you weren't one.

Please keep it that way.

With thanks and best wishes,
(whatever that's worth),

Your good friends and neighbours,
The People on Earth

A star is a large ball of gas that produces its own light and heat. The nearest star to us is the Sun. It's been calculated that every day about 8,640 stars across the Universe reach the end of their lives and explode, but this is only an estimate. The brightest and largest of the explosions are known as supernovas and these create more heat when they explode than our Sun will in its lifetime. In our galaxy, the Milky Way – and other galaxies of the same size – supernovas occur every 50 years or so. Supernovas are a good thing, though: their explosions spread star material across the galaxy, out of which our own planet was created.

## WHO HAD THE FIRST HOLIDAY?

Stressed from another busy week of repelling barbarians?
Can't face one more Senate debate about aqueduct building?
Unsure what to do with your remaining 130 feast days?
Then why not get away from it all . . . with a Pax Romana Holiday.

At Pax Romana Holidays, we have the break that's perfect for you.
Culture buffs can take in the sights on our Seven Wonders
of the Ancient World tour: see them now while they're still around!
If sport's more your thing, then why not head over to Greece

for our Olympic Games Holiday Special – it's just a hop,
skip and a jump away! Or, if you fancy something closer to home,
then choose from our range of stunning, luxury villas
in the fashionable resort of Baiae, with its incredible thermal baths.

And remember, subscribe to our Aurum Membership Package
and a small legion of Pax Romana reps will be with you every step of your journey –
to ensure you get to the holiday destination of your dreams
without being brutally murdered on the way.*

*Please note that this does not apply to our Visit Scotland holiday offer.

THIS WAY
COME AND SEE THE
7 WONDERS!
PAGES 36/37

We can't know precisely who had the first 'holiday', but what we do know is that the ancient Romans were among the first to take the whole business of going on holiday seriously. Not only did they take off a lot of days in celebration of their gods, or for festival days and emperors' birthdays, they were perhaps the first civilisation to travel for pleasure. In fact, a wealthy Roman family might do so for up to two years; let's hope they remembered to get someone to feed the cat while they were away.

# WHAT WAS THE BIGGEST GIFT EVER?

Three hundred and fifty sheets of copper and iron
In two hundred or so wooden crates,
Her journey ahead is more than three thousand miles
To where her new country awaits.

Nine years in the works, she must wait once again,
To be put back together afresh.
Funds need to be raised, and a pedestal built
On which she might finally rest.

When she does, she'll stand ninety-three metres tall
From the base to the tip of her torch,
And her seven-spiked crown will welcome the ships
As they enter the port of New York.

A gift to the nation from the people of France,
She is a symbol of freedom unfurled:
A hollow Colossus looking down on us all,
Liberty Enlightening the World.

The Statue of Liberty must certainly be a contender for the title of biggest gift ever. Ninety-three metres tall (equal to a 22-storey building) and weighing 204 tonnes (around the weight of 35 elephants), the statue was shipped in crates to New York from Paris in 1885 as a gift from the people of France to the USA. The intention was that the statue would become an international symbol of liberty, justice and democracy. The seven spikes of her crown represent the seven oceans and seven continents, and reinforce the statue's message of welcome to all.

## WHY DOES AN ONION HAVE LAYERS?

you're like an onion, she said,

and I said is that because
I, too, have many layers,
each one pushed out from the centre
to form a protective covering
over the bulb of my heart

and she said, not really,
she was talking about my papery skin,
and that occasional habit I had
of emitting a volatile gas
which would bring tears to her eyes

An onion, being a bulb, grows from a single bud at the base. The layers are created by the process of mitosis – the division of cells. As the new cells form, they push the older cells outward – creating new layers, which are effectively leaves. These layers are separated by smaller, thinner layers called membranes. Onions also contain a compound (something made from more than one element) that includes sulfur. When the onion is cut, this compound is released and reacts with the moisture in our eyes, making us cry. I'm tearing up just thinking about it.

## HOW MANY TIMES A DAY DO WE LAUGH?

Who'd want to be a grown-up?
It doesn't look much fun.
Three hundred times a day I laugh,
My teacher next to none.

No, I cannot keep a straight face.
Life's a constant **HOOT!**
I've laughed my socks off so much now,
I walk around barefoot.

That last verse didn't rhyme, did it?
Which makes me laugh some more –
I think I'll finish this one off
With a mighty old **GUFFAW!**

I must try not to **SPLIT MY SIDES**,
of which sometimes just the thought'll
be enough to make me **ROAR**,
**CRACK UP** or **SNORT** or **CHORTLE**!

But seriously, my poor teacher . . .
to help him with his struggle,
I've written him a 'ha-ku',
which I hope might raise a **CHUCKLE** . . .

**Ha ha ha ha ha**
**Ha ha ha ha ha ha ha**
**Ha ha ha ha ha**

It's true that, on average, children laugh hundreds of times more each day than adults. Estimates vary, but a child may laugh about 300 times a day, whereas an adult may laugh only 17 or 18 times a day. This is something I don't find very funny as laughter is good for you – it's scientifically-proven to lower our stress levels. Still, at least I'm doing better than a baby; it takes the average baby around three to four months to laugh, particularly at my jokes.

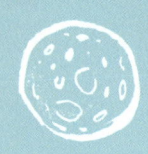

# WHICH IS THE BIGGEST COUNTRY IN THE WORLD?

It was announced that all existing systems of measurement were to be replaced with one that compared everything to the size of Wales.

'It's a very big day,' commented Dai Llewellyn, a spokesperson for the decision, estimating the day to be approximately three times the size of Wales.

Mr Llewellyn was quick to play down any unhappiness created by the decision, claiming the protesters were a minority – no bigger than a town the size of Porthcawl or Abergavenny.

However, a delegation from Russia, a country approximately 824 times the size of Wales, voiced its disapproval; as did a blue whale, the length of three Cardiff city buses,

who spouted his opinion that even the size of Wales itself would be better expressed in terms of 115 million blue whales or 2,861,974 football pitches, and he had enough data on that

to stretch to the Moon and back six times.

MEXICO

GREECE

PERU

Unsurprisingly, Wales is not the biggest country in the world; it just gets used a lot in the news as an indicator of size ('an asteroid the size of Wales' etc.), as do blue whales, double-decker buses, football pitches and the distance to the Moon and back. If we're measuring the biggest country in the world by *area*, it is indeed Russia, which tops the charts with a whopping 17 million square kilometres. If we're measuring in terms of *population*, however, then India comes out on top – with about 1.5 billion people, more than 450 times the population of Wales.

# ARE THE EGYPTIAN PYRAMIDS THE ONLY PYRAMIDS?

one of
the problems
of writing a poem
in the shape of a pyramid
is that if you forget the top line
then it all becomes a little bit pointless

If I had remembered to write the top line of my poem, I might have said that there are LOTS of other pyramids around the world. For example, there are more than 255 of them in Sudan, compared with the 100 or so in Egypt, and they can also be found in Italy, Greece, Mexico, Peru and Cambodia. Although I probably wouldn't have included all that because it would have taken up too much space. Also, if I had spent a little more time writing this poem, I might have realised that it's not actually in the shape of a pyramid (which is three-dimensional), it's in the shape of a triangle. But it's too late, I have written it now.

# HOW MUCH RUBBISH IS THERE AROUND EARTH IN SPACE?

Twinkle, twinkle, space debris,
I wonder how you came to be.
Up above the world so high,
Glittered litter in the sky.

Spacecraft that have broken down.
Satellites just floating round.
Rocket boosters long defunct,
Twinkle, twinkle, old space junk.

Nuts and bolts, discarded tools,
Adrift in space above us all.
Garbage bags and old paint chips,
The sky's a giant rubbish tip.

We've done our best to wreck the Earth,
Now space pollution's getting worse.
Let's clean it up A.S.A.P. –
Dwindle, dwindle, space debris.

We really need to clean up our act! It's estimated that there are more than 100 trillion untracked pieces of space junk in near-Earth orbit. While most of these may be tiny, there are still more than 23,000 objects larger than 10 centimetres. Some of these fall to Earth, too, from time to time: in 1997, a woman in Oklahoma got hit by part of a booster from a shuttle. It's no wonder that alien life forms have yet to make contact with us when they can see how messy we are.

## HOW MANY BONES DOES A BABY HAVE?

I've a bone to pick with you, the headmistress said.
I stood there and bowed my head,
staring silently at my shoes.

I waited for her to choose.
And while it's true I used to have more –
three hundred or so when I was newly born –
even now, with two hundred and six,
the options were numerous.

What would she pick? A tibia or fibula?
My scapula or sternum? A femur or humerus?
A metacarpal or metatarsal?
All those bones neatly wrapped up in the parcel of me . . .
but not a single one from my skeleton
could she settle on.

In the end, she picked the lot
then watched me as I flopped onto the floor.
On being excused, I oozed my way out
underneath her door.

It's true. We're at our boniest when we are babies – we have about 300 of them, in fact, compared with the approximately 206 bones we have by adulthood. That's because many of these bones fuse together over time. Some bones – such as the patella (kneecap) – take time to develop and only become proper bones when we reach the age of about ten. I could tell you more, but I thought I'd give you the bare bones of the answer.

## WHAT ARE NIGHTMARES?

I'll tell you
what a nightmare is

it's when you dream
you're trapped inside a snow globe
with no chance of escape

and then you wake the next day
all shaken up

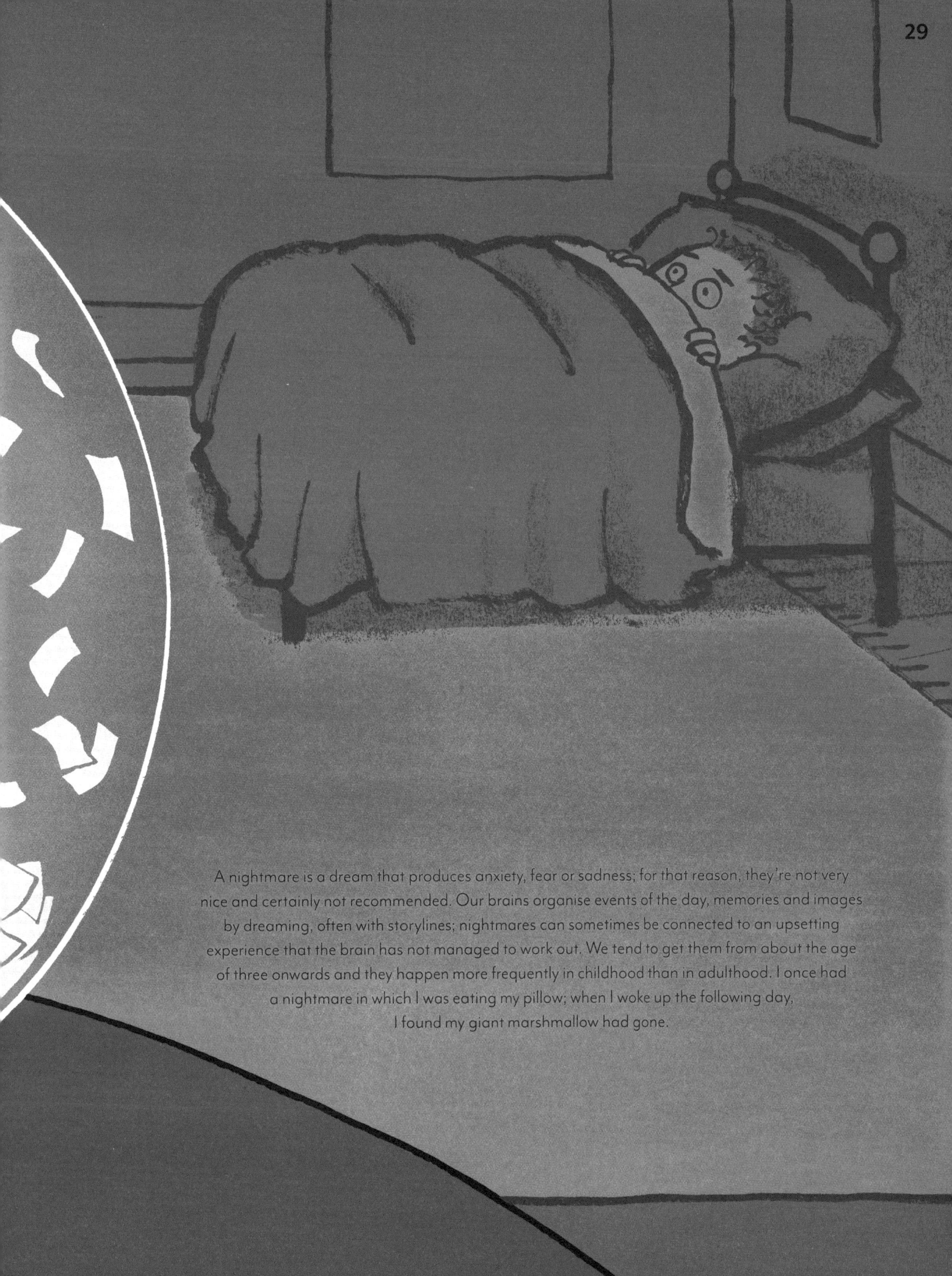

A nightmare is a dream that produces anxiety, fear or sadness; for that reason, they're not very nice and certainly not recommended. Our brains organise events of the day, memories and images by dreaming, often with storylines; nightmares can sometimes be connected to an upsetting experience that the brain has not managed to work out. We tend to get them from about the age of three onwards and they happen more frequently in childhood than in adulthood. I once had a nightmare in which I was eating my pillow; when I woke up the following day, I found my giant marshmallow had gone.

## WHY DO MY FINGERS AND TOES WRINKLE IN WATER?

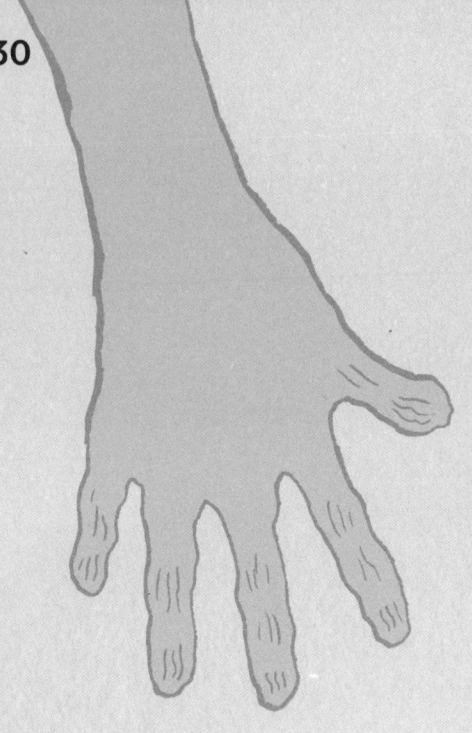

I lie in the bath
until the water turns cold
and when I look down,
I'm a hundred years old.*

I got wrinkly fingers,
I got wrinkly toes,
I'm a crinkle-cut crisp –
how quickly time goes!

I must have dropped off
for ten years at least.
I'd better get out –
it's time I de-creased.

*\* I'm not really so ancient —*
*that was a tiny untruth,*
*I've just washed off the oil*
*that keeps me waterproof.*

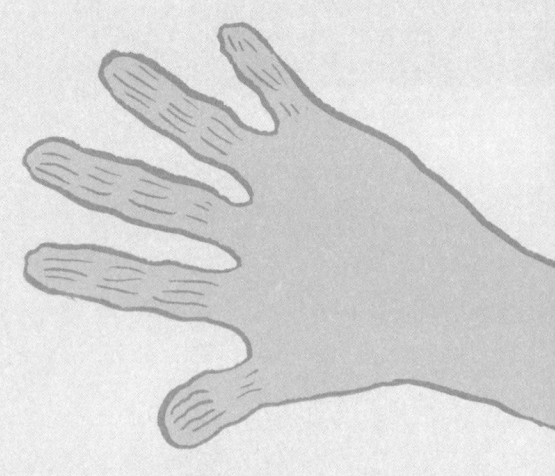

Fortunately, staying in the bath too long does not make us age prematurely. Those wrinkles that form on our skin are the result of the washing away of 'sebum' – an oil that covers the skin and makes it partly waterproof. Underneath the oil, we have a layer of dead keratin cells, which then absorbs the water and leads to wrinkling. We don't fully understand why this occurs, although some scientists think that it's an evolutionary reaction, giving humans better grip when handling or walking on wet objects. Other scientists think this theory doesn't quite hold water and that there are too many wrinkles in need of ironing out.

## WHY DON'T TREES BURST IN WINTER LIKE COLD PIPES?

Creak-groan-rustle-rustle-creak-groan-rustle-rustle-creak-groan-**KAPOW!**
Any ideas what that is?
That's the sound of an exploding tree.
Nasty business – or at least it would be, if that's what we did.

But you don't live as long as an oak tree –
I'll be a hundred and fifty next year (no birthday cake, thank you,
that amount of candles would freak me out) –
without learning a few tricks.

Now I don't want to get too technical with you
but it's all about pipe management.
Would you listen to me – I sound like a plumber!
But no, we have these pipes running through us, see,

and I don't need all that water running through them over the winter time
when I've got no interest in growing,
so what I do is draw it down to my roots,
then if my pipes want to expand or contract in the cold weather

they're free to do so without fear of exploding.
My bark's pretty helpful, too. It keeps me nice and warm.
Although it is worse than my bite!
Not really, that was a joke. Didn't work, though, did it.

Like the pipes in your house, trees have water running through them. A tree's pipes are called the xylem and phloem: xylem carries water from the roots to the leaves; phloem carries the food made by its leaves all around the tree. When water freezes, it expands; that's why you may sometimes get a burst pipe in your house. In winter, trees need less water and cleverly reduce the amount of water held in their pipes, drawing it down to the roots and eliminating the risk of their own pipes bursting.

# WHICH IS THE BIGGEST ANIMAL?

Six reasons why you rarely see a blue whale in the crowd at a football match:

1. Being by nature a solitary creature, the blue whale generally prefers to watch football from the comfort of its own armchair.

2. Catering facilities at most grounds are far from ideal, with most clubs unlikely to provide a sixteen-tonne krill pie at the half-time interval.

3. The powerful flippers of the blue whale are regarded as a health and safety risk, liable to result in large-scale casualties should a goal be celebrated.

4. The blue whale is discouraged from joining in the chants of fellow supporters, as its song is louder than a jet engine and would drown out all other noise for several miles around.

5. Club merchandise is often inadequate for blue whales: there is often a shortage of XXXXXXXXXXXXL shirts capable of stretching the length of its thirty-three metre body and it can take several years to knit one a bobble hat and scarf.

6. The blue whale has a reputation for being a passionate football fan who wears its heart on its sleeve. This can be problematic on match days given its heart weighs as much as a small car and contains blood vessels large enough for its fellow supporters to swim through.

Also, most football clubs frown upon blue whales attending their games as – being the largest animal that has ever lived on Earth – you could only fit three of them into a stadium. A female blue whale can weigh up to 190 tonnes and reach a length of over 33 metres. The largest land mammal is the African bush elephant, which weighs in at around a mere six tonnes; nothing compared to the blue whale but still heavy enough, however, to make it incapable of jumping.

## HOW DO CLOUDS WORK?

It's as if they form out of nothing,
a heavenly magic trick,
conjuring up wisps and ripples,
scruffy formations of fluff,
or impromptu gatherings of white, grey or black,
abracadabra, out of thin air,

rather than anything so sensible as science
and its vocabulary of evaporation,
saturation and condensation,
the inevitable result of sun upon water,
and the invisibility of gas rising and rising
until the air can contain it no more

and it becomes instead a quintillion jewelled droplets
clinging to the dust, floating in the sky,
a commonplace miracle, a cloud.

The sky contains invisible water vapour, which has evaporated from oceans, lakes, rivers and elsewhere. When the vapour becomes too heavy – which it will in cold air – it condenses into visible water droplets. These liquid water drops form on tiny particles such as dust that are floating in the air. The droplets are only around one-hundredth of a millimetre in diameter, but a large accumulation of the droplets becomes a cloud. If sunlight is equally scattered by the water droplets in a cloud, the cloud appears white; when clouds thicken, less sunlight can pass through them, and the cloud appears grey.
I would tell you more about the science of clouds, but it may just go over your head.

## WHY DO WE FART?

All the gas that we amass
should not be kept within, alas.
When its time comes to depart
that's what we like to call a fart,

also called a parp or squeak
(should it make your bottom speak),
or a simple toot of one's back horn –
to signal that the gas has . . . gorn.

Other terms you may come across:
ripper, fizzler, trouser cough,
grundle rumble, grunt and gurgler,
bottom burp and bumsen burner,

raspberry, stinker, whiffy wonder,
trumpton, thunder from down under,
wallop, fluff, benchwarmer, guff –
I think for now that's quite enough.

Remember, better out than in.
The fart is not embarrassing,
it's natural! But here's the thing:
do not do one before the King.

When we swallow food or drink, we swallow small amounts of air, which collect in our digestive system. Gases are also produced by the bacteria in our intestines that help us digest food. We can't keep all those gases inside us, so we let them out in the form of a fart or a burp: to the extent that we all burp or fart about 2.5 litres of gas each day. Thank you for reading this short fart-icle.

## WHAT WERE THE SEVEN WONDERS OF THE ANCIENT WORLD?

Everyone knows that! It's not much of a teaser.
For starters, there's the Great Pyramid of Giza
and that magnificent giant Statue of Zeus
(which stood in Olympia, if that's any use).
Then you've got the Hanging Gardens of Babylon –
please forgive me if I happen to babble on –
but another wonder that's not so hard to miss
is the ancient Greek Temple of Artemis.
And then who could forget the Colossus of Rhodes!
There's only two more, it's not like there's loads –
in Alexandria, the Lighthouse, built by Ptolemy
(the second pharaoh called that, if you still follow me).
Last up, Halicarnassus – the Mausoleum.
All gone but one, so you can no longer see 'em.

If you want to know which of the ancient wonders still exists, it's the Great Pyramid of Giza, which is also the oldest. It was built between 2700 and 2500 BCE to serve as a royal tomb. It's constructed from around two million stone blocks; so, if you have plans to build an exact replica, it's going to take you some time.

## ARE UNICORNS REAL?

In the cave, the unicorns were gathered together
to debate their own existence,
which had recently been much under question.

'Well, I certainly feel real,' said Fred, shaking his mane to prove it.
This statement was greeted by much nodding;
a few horns got bashed in the process.

'Yes, and I do, too!' snorted Angelina.
There was a universal stamping of hooves in agreement.
It was true! They absolutely did exist!

'So where are we going wrong then?' asked Geoff,
who had a reputation for being something of a neighsayer.
'Some humans don't believe in us.'

Denise thought she knew the answer.
'It's about marketing. We're simply not on people's radar.
We need to get ourselves out there a bit more.'

Dave had a suggestion. 'Start with the kids.
Their minds are always the most open to new ideas.
We just need to find ways of reaching them.'

'I'm thinking pencil cases, notebooks, backpacks,' shouted Wendy,
who had a background in branding and communication.
'You know, a sort of "Back to school" campaign.'

'Brilliant!' said Denise. But then she pulled a long face.
'It still feels as if we're missing something, though.'
The unicorns were quiet for a few minutes.

The silence was broken by a sharp bray from Chris.
'I know!' he said. 'Glitter! We need to be glittery!'
'Yes, that's it!' said Denise. 'And lots of bright vivid colours!'

They chattered excitedly about the new plans:
timelines, budget, responsibilities. All that is, except Colin.
When the cave was quiet again, he spoke up.

'I think we're over-complicating things,' he said.
'Wouldn't it be easier for us just to come out of hiding?
You know, to show ourselves again?'

'Don't you remember what happened to our friend the dodo?'
answered Denise. 'Or the quagga? The elephant bird?
The great auk? The atlas bear?'

After a short silence, a discussion began
concerning the branding of lunch boxes.

Some people might think that unicorns have never existed, but try telling that to the 'Siberian unicorn' (although this would be difficult since this ancient rhinoceros became extinct 39,000 years ago). Sure, it may have been 1.8 metres tall, over four metres long and weighed more than four tonnes, but it did have a single horn growing out of its head. And don't forget the narwhal either, which has claims to the title of 'unicorn of the sea'; quite frankly, it has a good point.

## WHEN WAS THE INTERNET BORN?

before the internet,
if you wanted to go surfing,
you would have to buy a wetsuit and a long, narrow-shaped board,
and find a beach with decent offshore winds
and long peeling waves

before the internet,
if you wanted to browse the web,
you would have to make friends with a spider
and be invited to inspect the delicate silver threads of its home

before the internet,
if you wanted to stream music,
you had to drop a CD or record into a small river

before the internet,
if you wanted to like someone's post,
you would have to write a note that said 'I really like this'
and tape it to one of the upright wooden supports in their garden fence

before the internet,
if you wanted to find out the answer to the question
'when was the internet born?',
you'd have to pay a visit to your local library
in order to consult an encyclopedia on one of its bookshelves,
but even then, you wouldn't be able to find out the answer,
because that was in the days
before the internet was born

It was more than 50 years ago, in the late 1960s, that an early version of the internet, called the ARPANET, was created for use by scientists and researchers. Over the next two decades, improvements were made to allow computers to communicate with each other around the world, but it wasn't until 1991 that a British programmer called Tim Berners-Lee created a 'web'. The World Wide Web allowed anyone on the internet to retrieve information, and it is what we use today; for instance, I used it just now to find out when the internet was born.

# HOW DEEP IS EARTH'S CRUST?

when I was seven years old,

I began to dig a hole in my backyard,
my plan:

1) shovel through the twenty miles of crust and eighteen hundred miles of impenetrable mantle

2) make my way through the planet's molten core, believed to be slightly hotter than the surface of the Sun

3) have a quick break for a bite to eat (cheese and pickle sandwich, packet of crisps)

4) crack on through the remaining mantle and crust

5) emerge blinking in triumph out the other side, somewhere in the region of Australia

looking back, it was a project always doomed to failure — I still replay the mistake I made — I should have used a bigger spade

Forty-one per cent of Earth's surface is covered by continental crust, which on average is around 40 kilometres thick. Its rocks date back four billion years. The remainder is covered by oceanic crust, which is a mere five to ten kilometres thick and about 170 million years old. Also, please note the impracticality of digging a hole straight down from the UK in the hope of coming out in Australia. Even if you could somehow develop the drilling technology to do so and withstand temperatures hotter than the surface of the Sun, you'd actually end up off the southeast coast of New Zealand.

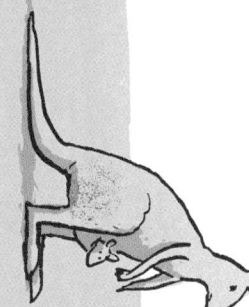

## WHICH ANIMALS HAVE MORE THAN ONE BRAIN?

We may think we're brainy, me and you,
but the cockroach has not one but two.

An achievement that, in turn, does pale
when considering the slug or snail,

the mosquito, squid, or bumblebee –
all of which, you see, have three.

But even that's not worth much fuss
when one observes the octopus –

with nine in total to show off
(two fewer than the silkworm moth).

But the winner, with none in easy reach –
with thirty-two, it's the **MIGHTY** . . .
the **EXTRAORDINARY** . . .
the **SUPER-BRAINY** . . .
**LEECH!**

BET YOU CAN'T SPOT ME ON PAGE 113

There are quite a few animals that have more than one brain. The octopus, for instance, has nine: a central one and then a mini-brain in each of its eight arms. The central brain is in overall charge, but the eight mini-brains can act independently to taste, touch and move. Rather clever, really, which makes it all the more surprising that you rarely see octopuses competing on TV quiz shows. The leech, though, is the champ. Its interior structure is divided into 32 segments, each with its own neuronal ganglia (groups of brain cells) and while these are all connected, they can also work independently.

## WHAT IS THE LARGEST SINGLE LIVING ORGANISM ON EARTH?

The vast forest
of Poseidon's ribbon weed
is waving gently
in the sea.

I wave back
only to realise it is waving
at the big shark
behind me.

The record is held by a meadow of *Posidonia australis* (a type of seagrass), also known as 'Poseidon's ribbon weed'. It's in Shark Bay off Western Australia, grows between 15 and 35 centimetres per year and is estimated to be around 4,500 years old. In other amazing plant news, a type of mushroom called *Armillaria ostoya* that grows in the Malheur National Forest in Oregon, USA, occupies seven square kilometres and is estimated to weigh nearly 32,000 tonnes, according to Guinness World Records. Rather excellently, it is known as the 'humongous fungus'.

## WHAT DOES GRAVITY DO?

Without gravity in a poem, lines can sometimes go astray.

It's often called light verse because the words will float away.

Add gravity to what you write –
the critics will be astounded!
Watch the words fall from your pen and keep your poems grounded.

Gravity is an invisible force that pulls objects towards each other. On our planet, gravity pulls everything down towards the centre of Earth, keeping us on the ground and causing things to fall. Without it, we – and everything else on Earth – would be floating in space! And did you know that the effect of gravity pushing us down all day causes our spines to shrink by about one centimetre? Our spines stretch out again when we're asleep, meaning we're at our tallest first thing in the morning when we wake up. Try measuring yourself to see.

## WHY CAN'T I ROLL MY TONGUE?

I'd tried and failed to roll my tongue
but I harboured one last hope –
so I went and found myself a hill
then rolled it down the slope.

It hurtled down at quite a lick –
it waggled and cried whheeeeeee!
I followed shortly afterwards,
'cos it was still attached to me.

Only 65 per cent of us can roll our tongues. It used to be thought that tongue rolling was genetic; you either had the gene to do it or did not. It's now believed, though, that you can learn how to tongue roll. Whether there's any point in learning it is another question; although if you have plans to compete in the World Tongue Rolling Championship, then you should probably give it a go.

# WHAT IS THE WORLD'S OLDEST INSTRUMENT?

Me hear noise one night in Cavern
Ogg hit boulder with big stick
Me ask Ogg what strange new sound is
Ogg say he call it rock music

Me carve flute from bone of cave bear
Me blow blow blow 'til mouth get sore
Me hear laugh – Stig say me useless
Stig got jazz bone flute grade four

Me form rock band with three others
We call ourselves Caveman Quartet
We write song and hope for stardom
But pop charts not invent just yet

Unsurprisingly, we don't know exactly what the oldest instrument was. It's likely to have been a drum, followed by a wind instrument of some kind, as many of the oldest discoveries have resembled flutes. One such find was a Neanderthal flute between 43,000 and 60,000 years old, carved from the thighbone of a young cave bear and, remarkably, it can still be played today. Some scientists claim, though, that it's simply a bone that has been chewed on by hyenas; which, if true, would be something of a blow.

# WHO CARVED THE FACES OF FOUR US PRESIDENTS IN A MOUNTAIN?

Mr Gutzon Borglum,
chief amongst carvers,
was not a sculptor
to do things by halvers.

For fourteen long years
he took up residence
on a mountain not entirely
without precedence.

When he had finished,
there were presidents (just four);
having taken his time,
not wanting to Rushmore.

In 1927, a sculptor called Gutzon Borglum began to carve the faces of four US presidents – George Washington, Thomas Jefferson, Abraham Lincoln and Theodore Roosevelt – into Mount Rushmore in the Black Hills of South Dakota. He didn't do it alone – there were 400 people who worked on the project, which took 14 years to complete. Before it was called Mount Rushmore, the Lakota Sioux called it Tunkasila Sakpe Paha (Six Grandfathers Mountain). It was a very important place for them and the monument remains controversial to this day.

## WHICH BIRD'S WINGS BEAT THE FASTEST?

Hush! Can you hear him as he nears,
the humble hummingbird?

That humming happens not because
he's forgotten all the words;

his tiny wings produce that sound
at eighty beats per second

and sometimes more than double that
or so it has been reckoned;

now look, he's resting on a branch –
is it any wonder why!

Heroic, humble hummingbird,
humdinger of the sky.

The hummingbird holds the record – or, to be more accurate, the ruby-throated hummingbird, with wings that beat at about 200 times per second. This takes up so much energy that the hummingbird spends a lot of time resting on branches. It's all rather impressive; unless, that is, you're a tiny midge of the genus *Forcipomyia*, which holds the insect record with 1,046 wing beats per second. I feel exhausted just thinking about it.

## WILL A GREAT WHITE SHARK EAT ME?

The problem is, I'm misunderstood.
It's the teeth, you see: they scare people.
I don't know whether that's because there's three hundred of them,
or because they're nearly three inches long,
or that they're as sharp as razors,
they just seem to unsettle people. Funny, really.

And then there's the issue of my fin.
'Menacing', one human called it. Menacing!
Sometimes I have to stick it up out of the water like that,
particularly when I'm near the beach
and on the look out for prey . . . sorry, not prey . . .
ice cream, I meant to say. Yeah, ice cream.

I blame that film. It's made people all nervy
whenever I'm . . . you know . . . doing a spot of surfing
or something. They start splashing around.
Screaming. Talk about an over-reaction!
And people are always doing the music from it.
Very cruel, if you ask me.

Yeah, sure, I do eat a few humans every year –
I am a shark after all, and you are rather tasty –
but believe me, I'm as friendly as the next guy.
I like to hang out and chill, not lash out and kill!
On the subject of which, I don't suppose
you happen to be free this afternoon?

Sharks get a bad press. Shark attacks on humans do happen – in 2022 there were
57 unprovoked attacks, only five of which were fatal. It's best to avoid the great white
shark, plus tiger and bull sharks, too, but most sharks are not considered dangerous.
Generally, sharks have far more to fear from people than we do from them.
The International Fund for Animal Welfare reports that more than
270 million sharks are killed by humans every year and
around 50 per cent of sharks are threatened with
extinction or near-extinction.

## HOW FAR AWAY IS MARS?

What's that? Where you goin', mate? Mars!
Oof. That's a bit of a trek, that is!
My advice is avoid the M25, 'specially
at this time of day. You'll be goin' nowhere fast!
Also, there's roadworks on the A12
so I'd keep away from that, too.

Your best bet, I reckon, is to wait
'til the year 2287. Late August if you can –
Mars'll be a bit closer to Earth then, see,
only about 34 million miles away
though I'd still do yourself a packed lunch,
those interstellar service stations

are a right rip-off – £5.20 for a cheese sandwich!
Nah, 'cos if you go at this time of day,
Mars is about 220 million miles from Earth
and that's a fair old slog, that is,
'specially when you've got little ones.
Hope they don't get rocket-sick!

Why you all headin' there anyway –
holiday, is it? Don't think it's rained there
for a few million years so you should be okay.
Oh right, sorry mate, you're off back home!
I thought you looked a bit green
Should've guessed by the antennae.

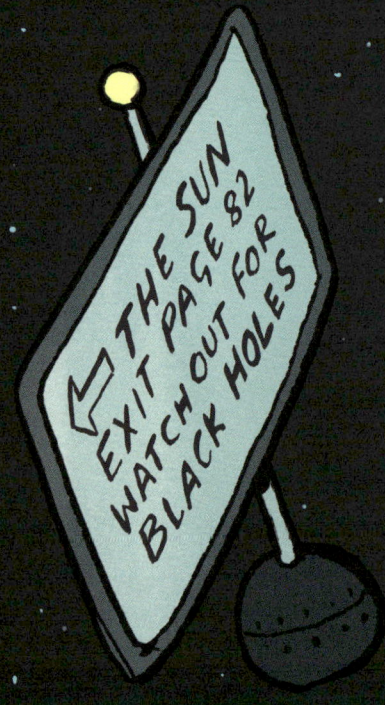

The distance of Mars is something of a moving target because both Earth and Mars are busy orbiting (moving around) the Sun. The average distance between the two is about 225 million kilometres, but this can vary a lot. Astronomers have calculated that Mars will be at its closest approach to Earth for 600 years on 29 August 2287, when it will be a mere 55,688,458 kilometres away. While that still might seem like quite a distance, it's a little bit more convenient than Neptune, say, which is nearly 4.5 billion kilometres from Earth, according to NASA. There's not even a direct shuttle service.

## WHY DO PEOPLE HUG?

Heard the news? HUGE, if true – being hugged is good for you.

For nothing works quite like a cuddle if you want to un-befuddle.

A chemical's released, you see, which helps reduce anxiety.

So come here, then, and nestle close in – let's get our dose of oxytocin.

When we hug (or exercise), our bodies release a hormone called oxytocin. This is a chemical messenger that makes us feel warm and fuzzy inside and can help us to feel safe and secure or calm. It is important for human behaviour – it helps to strengthen the bond between people and improve communication between friends and family members. Oxytocin can also help stop us feeling stressed and sometimes gets called the 'cuddle chemical'. We could all do with a bit of that in our lives.

## CAN YOU SEE THE GREAT WALL OF CHINA FROM SPACE?

The Sun rises and sets sixteen times a day
as we hurtle serenely around you;
every ninety minutes, a new orbit begins.
This space station is far from stationary.

The sight of you is dizzying:
you are no ordinary lump of rock.
From the swirls of your oceans to the sweep
of your forests, you still shout life.

Your poles may be shrinking
but the colours of the aurora continue to dance,
while at night, the cities light up
like the constellations themselves.

From here where I sit, it is not possible
to see what else we have made,
all I can see is what we might lose,
as we go round in circles once more.

Unfortunately you can't see the Great Wall of China from space. In fact, you can't see any human-made objects from space without special equipment. If you have a camera with a zoom lens, things get a bit better; you might be able to make out the Pyramids of Giza, although the Great Wall remains difficult to spot, given that it's long, winding and thin. And should you ever find yourself staring out of the window of the International Space Station, you may well see rivers or forests or shining city lights but probably not me, here, waving up at you, hoping you might be waving back.

## HOW DID THE ANCIENT EGYPTIANS MAKE A MUMMY?

First, take the body into a tent,
closing the tent flaps securely behind you
so no one can see what you are up to.

Wash the body in palm wine
then rinse with water from the Nile,
while trying not to think about what comes next.

Using a nearby brain hook,
draw out the brain through the nostrils.
Attempt unsuccessfully not to throw up.

Remove and wash the stomach,
intestines, liver and lungs. Pack them in salt
and store in four canopic jars.

Please remember: on no account
should the heart be removed
as this is essential for the afterlife,

and besides, you'll have had more than enough
of removing internal organs
by this stage anyway.

Stuff the body and cover with salt
and leave to dry out. Do your homework
or play a game of knuckle bones.

After forty days, stuff the body
with linen or sand to give it a more human shape.
Use recycled materials where available.

After seventy days, wash the corpse
and wrap in fine linen bandages, placing
amulets and papyri between the layers –

that journey to the afterlife is well tough,
full of peril, so your mummy is
gonna need all the help it can get.

Use glue to hold everything together
(no sticky tape, please) then paint eyes and face
but only if you're quite good at art.

Place in the decorated coffin
you hopefully remembered to make earlier.
If not, you'd better make one now.

Good luck to your mummy on its journey!
And remember, before embarking on the above,
do check the subject is dead first.

Sorry about the above but there's no getting around it – making mummies was a gory business. The ancient Egyptians made mummies because they believed a person's soul would need to recognise its body when it reached the afterlife. In order to do so, the body would have to be preserved in as lifelike a way as possible. Hence all that business above, which again I apologise for – although I'm just telling you what they used to do, so don't blame me.

# IF A COIN FELL FROM THE EMPIRE STATE BUILDING, WOULD IT KILL YOU?

### NO!

To get down to specifics,
it's all about physics.

You see, a coin       dropped

from the tower
would reach no more than
300 kilometres per hour.

But throw in air resistance
and the existence
of an updraft

and the very question itself
seems rather daft –

the coin's
terminal velocity
would not be enough
to cause
an atrocity.

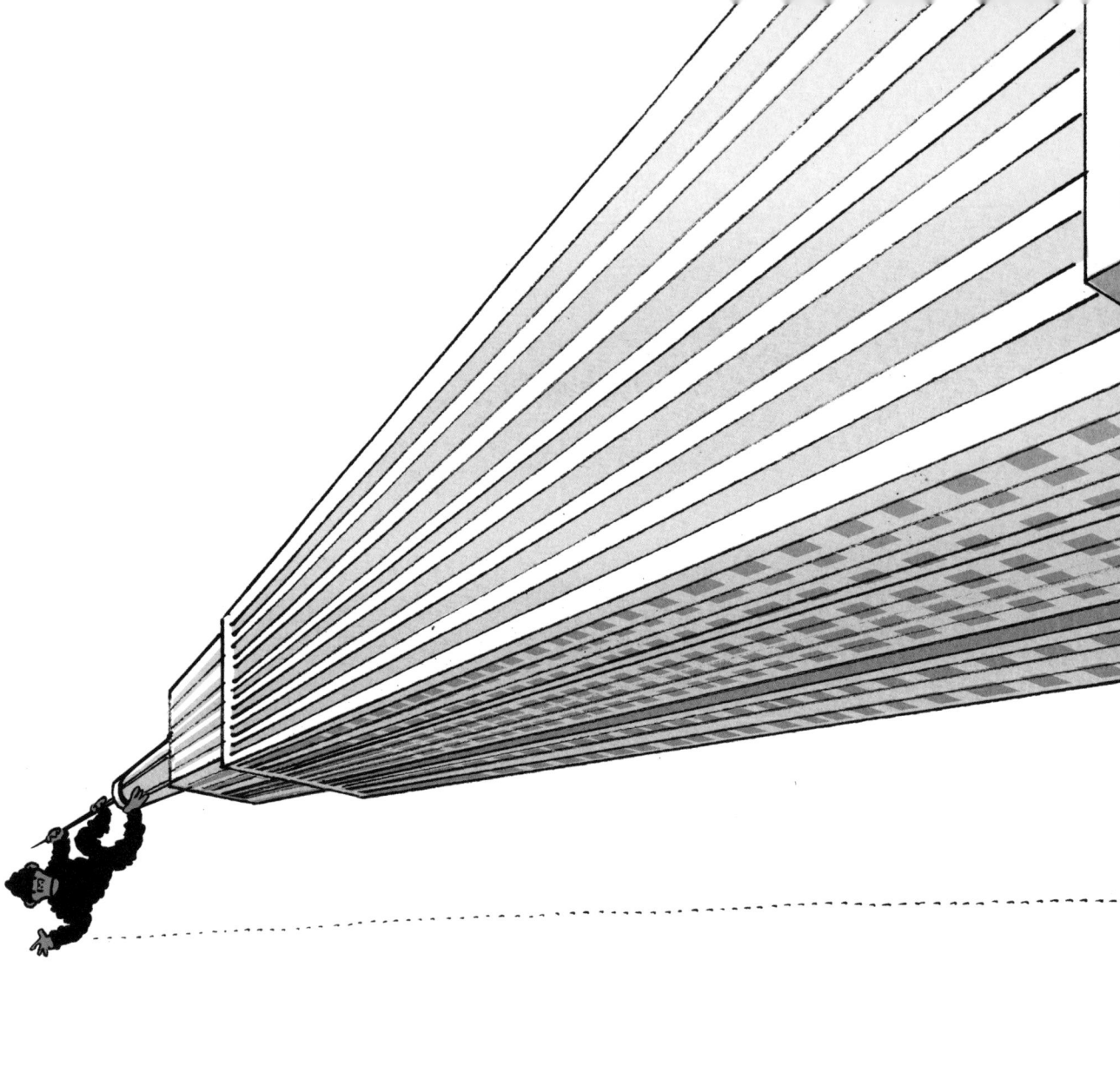

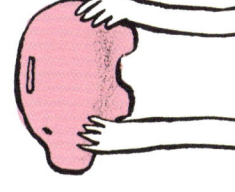

Of course, if you don't believe the physics, we could always toss this coin to decide the answer – heads is yes, tails is no.

**TAILS!** That proves it! I told you so.

What do you mean, you don't believe me? Don't try this yourself – instead, let me explain once more. Physics shows us that a coin dropped from the Empire State Building, which is 380 metres high, could potentially reach a speed of about 300 kilometres per hour. If you factor in air resistance, however, it slows to a 'terminal velocity' of about 100 kilometres per hour, making it very unlikely to penetrate someone's skin. By way of comparison, a .22 calibre bullet has an initial speed of around 960 kilometres per hour. Do you believe me now? Good. I'm glad to see the penny has finally dropped.

# COULD A WOMAN BE A GLADIATOR?

A lion tells all:

Well, as far as I recall, they absolutely could.
And some of them were very good.
One I remember, in particular . . .
it may have been in the reign of Caligula . . .
Achillea, I think her name was.
Out she'd come and **BIFF! BASH! BOSH!** –
limbs and carcasses all over the floor!
The stench! The savagery! The gore!
I doubt there's been such carnage
since the destruction of Carthage.
That last time she went into the arena,
she killed a leopard, two boars, and a hyena
before strangling an alligator.

Yes, I was glad I ate her.

It's true – there were some women gladiators in ancient Rome, although there weren't very many of them. Their proper name was gladiatrix (singular) or gladiatrices (plural). Like the male gladiators, they would fight, hoping to win their freedom but often losing their lives instead. In 200CE, Emperor Septimus Severus outlawed women from fighting in the area, but there's evidence that the practice continued for some time afterwards.

# HOW DO PLANES FLY UPSIDE DOWN?

To prevent you feeling scared and nervy
When you're flying above the Earth,
An important thing's
To have aerofoil wings —
You can even journey topsy-turvy.

If, for some reason unclear to me, you fancy flying upside down, it helps to have a plane with aerofoil wings. These wings have a curved upper surface and a flatter lower surface. They help to deflect the air and alter the air pressure above and below the plane to create an upward force called 'lift'. When a plane's nose is up and its tail is down, enough lift is produced by the wings to flip it upside down.

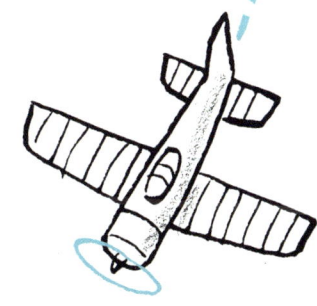

## HOW MANY TEETH DOES A CROCODILE HAVE?

And good morning to you, Mrs O'Dile.
Do make yourself comfortable in the chair,
open those jaws nice and wide,
and we'll take a look at them, shall we?

Gosh, that IS a big mouth. Wonderful.
What an incredible set of gnashers!
I've never seen anything like them before!
So let's check if all is in order . . .

They do seem to be in good nick.
I would say, though, that you do have rather more teeth
than I'm used to seeing in my patients, Mrs O'Dile.
I count sixty-six in total, that's about double.

They're sharper and pointier, too.
A few teeth appear to have decayed or fallen out
but remarkably it appears
there are new ones coming through.

I'm sorry, what's that, Mrs O'Dile?
You've been experiencing some pain?
Any idea which one? What? You'd like me
to climb in and take a closer look.

That's not generally considered normal practice
but I suppose, on this occasion,
it might be rather helpful . . . okay, I'm in . . .
now, if I could just ask you, Mrs O'Dile,

to keep your mouth wide open while I . . .
Mrs O'Dile, please can you keep your mouth open?
It's rather dark in here. Mrs O'Dile?
Mrs O'Dile! **MRS O'DILE! MRS O'** –

A Nile crocodile has between 64 and 68 sharply pointed teeth. When its teeth fall out or decay, new teeth take their place; on average, a crocodile's chompers are replaced every 20 months throughout their life. Humans' bite force is around 160psi (pounds per square inch) but a crocodile's is around 5,000psi. With that strength they can easily crush a turtle shell, or even the skulls of its prey. All of this research has really highlighted to me the benefits of not finding myself between a crocodile's jaws.

## WHERE IS THE HOTTEST PLACE ON EARTH?

I thought I'd write a poem
in a place called Furnace Creek
some said the spot
could get quite hot
more than fifty at its peak

the temperature was soaring
so I wrote at quite a clip
the sun was strong –
before too long
my lines began to drip

words that once were solid

now down the page had run

my thoughts expressed

a total mess

allmeltedinthesun

On 16 August 2020, Furnace Creek in Death Valley, California, USA, reached a whopping 54.4°C, the highest air temperature ever recorded. Surface temperature can get even higher: the Sonoran desert along the Mexico / USA border has recorded one of 80.8°C. Definitely not jumper weather. Given the effects of global warming, it's very likely we'll see these temperatures beaten again in the coming years; records that we really don't want to be breaking.

# WHAT IS A PRIMARY COLOUR?

Do take a seat, Mr Brown.
And thank you very much for your application
for a position in our Primary Colours Department.

I wonder if you could tell us what you feel
you might bring to the role? I see. You're very prominent
in natural settings. Any examples of that for us?
Ah, yes, trees. And soil. Most bears and horses.
Potatoes. Excellent, most excellent.

Tell me, any experience of working in a rainbow?
Not directly, although you do see yourself
as a darker shade of orange? Ah, right.
That's good to know; very useful, indeed.

And what would you say is your greatest strength?
You're solid and dependable, yet flexible.
In what way, flexible? Ah, I see. You can vary from beige
and caramel through to walnut and smoky topaz?
That's terrific, it really is. Absolutely splendid.

I'm afraid, though, that's not quite what we're looking for
here in the Primary Colours Department.
What we're really after here is someone completely unique,
who can combine with colleagues
to cover pretty much the whole spectrum.

Mrs Blue over there, for instance. Or opposite her,
Mr Yellow. Honestly, you should see what happens
when the two of them put their heads together!
Talking of which, have you met Mrs Green?
She's an important member of our Secondary Colours Department.

In fact, let me take you down to meet her now.
I think she's got a vacancy in her section; I'd have thought
someone with your particular skill set would be perfect.

Not at all, Mr Brown; only too glad to help!
And no more of this 'Mrs Red' business, please.
Call me Ruby.

A primary colour is the starting point for mixing other colours. The typical primary colours used for painting are red, yellow and blue. These can be mixed together to create secondary colours, such as purple, made by mixing red and blue. But it's actually more complicated than that. Our eyes take in coloured light differently to colours of materials such as paints. Because of this, electronic devices that produce coloured light use red, green and blue as their primary colours, to make the images you see on their screens. My own favourite colour is green; I love it as much as blue and yellow combined.

# WHY DOES THUNDER RUMBLE?

Somebody stole my thunder
It happened late last night
I'd been underneath my duvet
Hiding there in fright

I last heard it moments after
That final lightning flash
Its sound made as the air expands
Then suddenly contracts

The lightning bolts have bolted, too
Stormed off at half past one
I wonder where my thunder went
The mystery rumbles on

Thunder is the sound of lightning, which is caused by electricity building up inside clouds until it needs to be released. Lightning quickly heats up the air around it – the air then cools quickly after the lightning flash. This rapid heating and cooling creates the rumbling sound of lightning – the one that makes me hide under my duvet whenever I hear it. You can estimate how far away lightning is by timing how many seconds later you hear the thunderclap – about three kilometres for every ten seconds.

## HOW DID BEETHOVEN COMPOSE MUSIC WHEN HE WAS DEAF?

Inside my head, they take their seats
and the music comes alive,
each note and phrase and harmony
in the orchestra of my mind.

I journey on the road to joy,
each touch answers with a sound –
my imagination is a symphony,
in which everything's allowed.

In 1810, when Beethoven composed his most famous piano piece, 'Für Elise', he was 39 years old and almost completely deaf. He was not born deaf, however, so when his hearing started to go, he had already developed such a great knowledge of music that he knew how notes and chords fitted together and the sounds they would make. For a while, he also used ear trumpets and other devices, sometimes holding a pencil in his mouth and resting it against the piano. The vibrations created by the piano meant he could 'feel the sounds'.

# HOW MANY ASTRONAUTS HAVE GONE TO THE MOON?

I get lonely sometimes, stuck up here –
it's rather dull with not much atmosphere,
and while the stars try hard to comfort me,
I moon around and hope for company.

But it wasn't always as quiet as this,
if you would let me gently reminisce –
there was a time when you could barely move
for humans walking in my grooves

or taking samples from my craters.
Twelve walked upon my surface. But later
all that stopped. No more dramatic touchdowns,
no boots bouncing lightly on my ground.

That first small step had been a giant leap
for me as well – but now I am left to sleep
and dream about the time when I, perhaps,
did briefly find myself on the map.

And, one night, should you look up at me,
when you feel all alone in the galaxy,
remember I know what that feels like, too –
come back and see me. I'll be waiting for you.

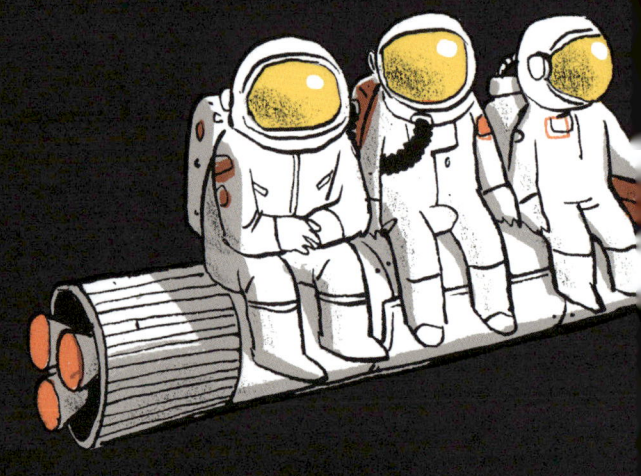

A grand total of 12 astronauts have visited the Moon, beginning with Neil Armstrong and Buzz Aldrin in July 1969. All have been from the USA. It's been a while, though, since anyone went there; 1972 was the last landing: or, as the old saying goes, 'once in a blue moon'.

# IS ZILLION A REAL NUMBER?

If I've told you once,
I must have told you
a zillion squillion gazillion times,
don't exaggerate.

And don't make up numbers, either.

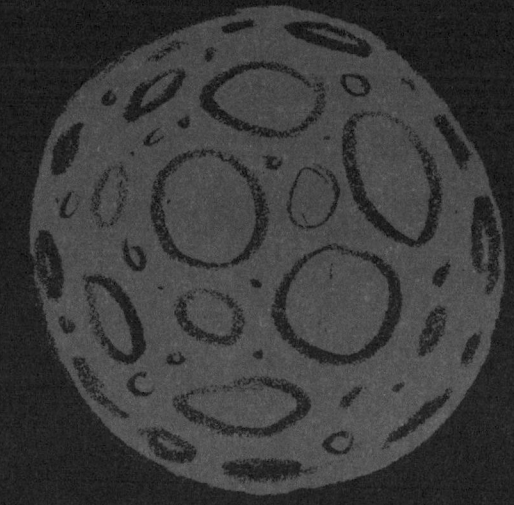

No, zillion is not a real number. And neither is squillion or gazillion. But these words do get used in a more general sense to express a very large number, often when exaggerating. Here are some numbers that are real: trillion (12 zeros), quadrillion (15 zeros), octillion (27 zeros) and decillion (33 zeros). These are teeny compared to a googol, though, which has 100 zeros, or a googolplex, which is a number larger than the number of atoms in the Universe. So quite large, really, and a number you're unlikely to count up to when you're trying to get to sleep at night.

# WHY DOES MILK GO BAD?

the milk went bad
and embarked upon a life of crime and cream,
got mixed up in all kinds of schemes –
arson, fraud, theft, the lot! –
but soon things turned sour
for the stupid clot
when he got caught in the act,
a bungled burgle
which saw him fall at the final curdle

the next day, before the judge
(lactose intolerant and very superior),
the milk tried to blame it
on the bacteria

having semi-skimmed the evidence,
the judge pronounced a verdict of guilty
with a sentence
that could not have been crueller –
three and half years back in the cooler.

Milk goes off if the surrounding temperatures rise high enough for bacteria to grow. The rise in acidity that the bacteria produces will sour the milk and cause it to form lumps called 'curd'. Ugh. There's nothing worse than taking a big spoonful of cornflakes and finding the milk has gone bad: those creamy lumps are really hard to chew.

# IS THERE A MONSTER IN LOCH NESS?

I've been carved in stone by ancient Picts
And captured in all sorts of pics
It's no wonder then that I feel miffed
To find out that I don't exist

I think it to be very mean
Given all the times that I've been seen
To then discover that I've never been
It plays havoc with my self-esteem

I've heard some say that I'm a seal
Or perhaps a kind of giant eel
**MONSTROUS** is how it makes me feel
Oh, how I wish that I was real

I really want there to be a monster in Scotland's Loch Ness, but there's no real evidence to suggest there is, and that's after a lot of surveys and underwater explorations of the loch (lake). None of that stops the rumours, though, or the claimed sightings of 'Nessie', which number more than 4,000 and date back to 1,500 years ago. The most famous photograph of Nessie was taken in 1934, with what looks like the monster's small head and neck poking out of the water. But I think this was almost certainly a hoax, and my good friend the Yeti agrees with me.

## WHAT'S INSIDE A TENNIS BALL?

Should you wonder why these words are here, high above the others, it's because I've filled them up with air and written them in rubber. I bounced them on the line below, which I think is rather neat . . .

because this is concrete poetry and this line is the concrete.

The core of a tennis ball is made from a layer of natural rubber, inside which air or gas is pressurised to around 27psi (pounds per square inch) to give the best bounce. A friend of mine once had a dog who was obsessed with tennis balls, and would always carry one around in his mouth. He told me that his dog was capable of retrieving a tennis ball from more than a kilometre away, but I think that sounds far-fetched. Concrete poetry, by the way, is when a poem's words are arranged to create a visual image that helps to reinforce the subject of a poem – and, in the case of my poem above, to give words more 'bounce'!

## DID DINOSAURS HAVE FEATHERS?

Recently, I've been tracing back my family tree.
Checking out my ancestry,
following us chickens deep in time,
way, way back through our family line.
Or the pecking order, as I like to call it.

Anyhow, I found an answer I did **NOT** expect –
seems like I'm related to the T. rex!

I know, right? That was a bit of a shocker.
I mean, us chickens descended from that rotter?
Can't see the resemblance myself.
But then I learnt something else –
so, apparently it turns out
that guy even had feathers just like us!

As you can imagine, it caused quite a fuss
back in the coop. These things do.

I still can't get over it. Not sure I'll ever!
I tell you, you could have knocked me down . . .
well . . . with a feather.

It would appear that some dinosaurs did have feathers! It's now thought that several dinosaurs, from the crow-sized Microraptor to the huge Tyrannosaurus (also known as T. rex) and Allosaurus, had some sort of feathery covering. This might have been for display, to regulate body temperature, for camouflage and defence, or for waterproofing. Perhaps we shouldn't be so surprised given that birds are the only remaining descendants of dinosaurs. And here's another thing: birds such as the ostrich and the chicken are indeed the closest living relatives to the Tyrannosaurus: cluck cluck ROAR!

## WHY DOES MY HEART BEAT?

It's the sound the heart makes as it's pumping out blood.
Is that any good?

What, you would like a little more? Why, sure.

The heart has four chambers – two atria and two ventricles.
When the muscular walls of your heart's right atrium are full
with oxygen-poor blood from all over your body, they contract,
squeezing the blood through a one-way valve into your right ventricle.
When your ventricle is full, its walls contract and squeeze the blood
out of your heart via another one-way valve to your lungs.

I hope you are still following this.

In your lungs, carbon dioxide and other waste products are removed
and fresh oxygen is added to the blood. This flows into your left atrium,
which contracts and pumps the blood into your left ventricle, which pumps
the oxygen-rich blood into your aorta and out to the rest of your body.

Do be aware, I shall be testing you later.

The heartbeat is completed and everything rests for a moment, then the blood
travels to every cell in your body. Veins carry the oxygen-poor blood
back to your right atrium, and the whole cycle starts again.
Oh, just to add that your heart's electrical system controls the rate and rhythm
of the heartbeats and supplies your body with the right amount of blood
at the correct rate that it needs to work well.

What's that, too much detail?

You do realise, don't you, that you're going to have to do all of that
approximately one hundred thousand times every day –
in fact, in the time it's taken you to read this far,
your heart should have beaten at least one hundred times,
so it is worth getting your head around.

Or your heart, for that matter.

As you can see from the above, this is a subject very close to my heart. We have around five litres of blood in our body, but the heart pumps around 7,500 litres worth each day. It's amazing I find the time to do anything else.

## WHERE IS THE DEEPEST PLACE IN EARTH'S OCEANS?

You'd think it would be safe down here
in the deep silence of this trench,
a wide, wild world of weird beauty,
but even here, there's no defence

from what it is you do up there,
those unfathomable miles above.
A place too remote to hear our cries
but enough, we say. ENOUGH!

Who am I? *Eurythenes plasticus*,
a mere shrimp, of no fixed purpose –
named after what was found in me
ten thousand metres beneath the surface.

In the western Pacific Ocean between Guam and the Philippines, south of Japan, lies the Mariana Trench. The bottom of the southern end of the trench is called the Challenger Deep. It is nearly 10,935 metres below sea level and is the deepest point known on Earth. In 2020, a shrimp-like species discovered in the trench was found to have eaten microplastics and was given the name *Eurythenes plasticus* to highlight the problem. How deep is the ocean? Not deep enough, it would seem, to get away from what we humans are doing to this planet.

# WHAT IS THE DIFFERENCE BETWEEN AN EMIGRANT AND AN IMMIGRANT?

It's a matter of direction.

An emigrant seeks a new homeland
and leaves their world behind.

And an immigrant is what you are
when you finally arrive.

What then is a refugee?

That's someone forced to leave their home,
who cannot stay there any more,

and seeks out safety, far away
from persecution, famine, war.

But tell me, who then is a refugee?

The answer's simple.
It could be you; it could be me.

There are lots of reasons why people might emigrate, leaving their country in search of another: to find work; to escape poverty; to join family; to receive better education; to escape war, persecution, political instability, famine or natural disasters caused by climate change. At the end of 2023, there were around 117 million people who had been forced to leave their homes, or run the risk of being killed or imprisoned or persecuted. Even more shockingly, around 40 per cent of these displaced people were children.

# HOW DOES A HONEYBEE BUILD ITS HIVE?

I may not be Pythagoras
Or Archimedes,
But when I'm making a hive,
I'm the bee's knees.

Yeah, move over, honey –
I'm producing some wax.
My mind's all abuzz
With the beauty of maths.

You see, it's all about shape
When you're making a hive –
For it has to be strong
If it's going to survive.

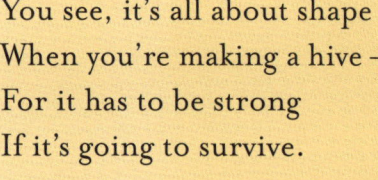

And I'm a B+ student
At Honeybee Academy,
Because the hives that I make
Are nice and hexagony.

Bees build their hives with hexagons, one of the strongest mathematical shapes. Hexagons fit together perfectly with no gaps, making hives very efficient structures. It's a good job they do build so efficiently because a honeybee has to consume around eight kilograms of honey to produce just one kilogram of wax. What's more, it would take 12 honeybees their entire lifetime to make one teaspoon of honey, and it takes the nectar from two million flowers to make a 450-gram jar of honey. It's a very labour-intensive 'beesness'.

# WHY DO THINGS FLOAT?

That wood floats but a rock will sink
is the kind of thing that makes me think:
for, on the surface, it makes no sense
until you know a rock's more dense,
its molecules more tightly packed,
no way for air to end up trapped,
whereas wood is not as dense as water
so bobs around just like it oughta.

Having figured out that must be it,
I feel quite buoyant, I must admit.

It's all about density. All objects are made up of small particles called molecules. These may be packed close together or spread out. The closer they are together, the more dense the object is. Objects that are more dense than water will sink in it; objects that are less dense will float. Archimedes, an ancient Greek mathematician and inventor (c.287–211BCE), also helped us understand why things float. While having a bath, he worked out that as the weight of his body was pushing down on the water, the water was also pushing back against him. This pushing force of water against an object is called buoyancy. It was his 'Eureka' moment; or at least it would have been had he actually shouted that word on coming up with the discovery.

## HOW FAR AWAY IS THE SUN?

Welcome aboard this Icarus Airlines flight to the Sun.
We wish you a safe and pleasant journey with us today.
With an average speed of about 650 kilometres an hour,
we estimate our flight time to be approximately twenty years,
although we will try to make up a few hours along the way.

A trolley service is available on this flight, serving
a range of hot and cold food; although, frankly, most of it will
become increasingly hot as we near our destination.
Choose from a wide selection of films, television programmes
and games on our inflight entertainment system,

then choose again and again and again and again
until you've watched Home Alone 2 three hundred times
and know every single line of every TV show and movie.
You can also use your screens to check out the Flight Map
to see where we are on our 150-million-kilometre journey.

To help keep you cool, this Icarus Airlines Flight 240
has been fitted with a state-of-the-art air-conditioning system,
although passengers should be aware that when we get
within a few million kilometres of our destination,
there is a strong likelihood of the plane being vaporised . . .

But there's absolutely no need to sweat about that now.
Strap in, sit back and enjoy your journey with Icarus Airlines.
It's reported that the Sun will be something of a scorcher today,
with temperatures reaching 15 million degrees Celsius in its core.
Hope you've not forgotten to pack your sun cream!

---

Given that Earth moves around the Sun, there is not a definitive answer – it depends where we are in our orbit. The average distance, though, is nearly 150 million kilometres. At this distance, light takes eight minutes and 19 seconds to reach Earth. Don't be alarmed but we're slowly moving away from the Sun. When the Sun burns fuel, it loses power, mass and gravity, so its gravitational pull on Earth is gradually weakening and we're moving away from it by about 15 centimetres every year. Like I say, it's nothing to worry about but worth keeping an eye on.

"WHOOPS! I THINK WE TOOK A WRONG TURN AT PAGE 50."

## WHAT IS A BLACK HOLE?

To be honest with you,
this wasn't really a question
I thought I'd be particularly interested
in writing a poem about


but – not quite appreciating
the gravity of the situation –
I found myself feeling strangely attracted to it
and eventually got sucked in.

A black hole is a region of space that nothing, not even light, can escape from, because gravity is so strong there. It results in a huge amount of mass being concentrated in a very small area. Most black holes form when there has been a collapse of a massive star – a supernova – at the end of its life. The star implodes, its centre collapsing under its own weight to form the black hole. Every large galaxy has a supermassive black hole in its centre that is capable of eating entire planets and stars. In our galaxy, the Milky Way, the supermassive black hole is called Sagittarius A*, and it has a mass equal to about four million Suns. According to NASA, it would fit inside a ball so large that it could hold a few million Earths.

# HOW LONG CAN YOU SURVIVE IN A DESERT IF YOU DRANK YOUR OWN PEE?

There was a young woman called Clara
Who found herself in the Sahara
She drank her own pee
But discovered that she
was only getting more dehydrated and so she asked if I could introduce
a camel into the story who might carry her out of this limerick altogether
and take her to a shop to get herself a big bottle of water – which I did –
and it wasn't long before she felt much better and I realised that this
wasn't even a poem any more so I stopped writing it.

Don't drink your own pee! Trying this when you have no water does not save you from dehydration. In fact, it will just dehydrate you faster – and the more dehydrated you become, the higher the concentration of pollutants in your pee will be. Also, I can imagine it doesn't taste very nice. If you do find yourself without water in a desert, you'd be better off collecting dew or searching for green vegetation and then digging for water beneath it. Or going to a local supermarket, if you can find one.

# WHAT IS A RIGHT ANGLE?

To stop you getting in a right tangle,

The answer is that it's one of these
i.e. an angle of 90 degrees.
You'll find one in the corner of a square;
a cute thing of which to be aware.

this poem serves as a brief example.

An angle is formed when two straight lines meet. An angle of exactly 90 degrees is called a right angle. They're always knocking about in the corner of squares and rectangles. They're very useful things, particularly when building as right angles have a lot of strength and can hold up weight effectively. Please note that angles of other degrees (for example, 52 degrees or 127 degrees) are not right angles; in fact, in the context of this question, they are wrong angles.

# WHO INVENTED FOOTBALL?

The boy done good.
Or the girl, we don't really know

but whoever they are,
they've gone out there and invented their socks off,

put in a big shift, given it 110 per cent,
used their noggin to come up with an idea,

kicked it around a bit with their mates
(because at the end of the day, it's all about teamwork)

and then they've got the idea back
and just run with it, at pace,

**TWISTING**

**AND TURNING**

**AND SHIMMYING**

until the space has opened up in front of them
and they've thought 'right, maybe I'll have a pop'

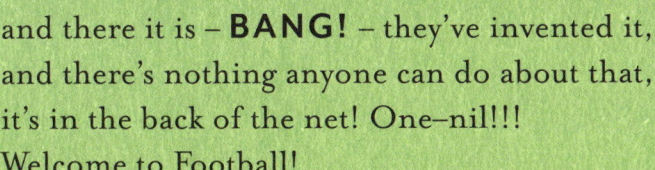

and there it is – **BANG!** – they've invented it,
and there's nothing anyone can do about that,
it's in the back of the net! One–nil!!!
Welcome to Football!

I mean, you really couldn't write a script like this.
It's top, top inventing, it really is.

It seems unlikely that any one person invented football. It's been around for a long time: the game of 'cuju' in China 2,000 years ago was very similar in nature, for instance. In 1314, the Lord Mayor of London banned 'football' in the city as it was causing 'chaos'. In 1863, Ebenezer Morley, a founder of the Football Association, helped to establish the laws of the game, which have remained the same ever since – except for the introduction of corner kicks, offside, substitutes, penalty shoot-outs, the back-pass rule and VAR (video assistant referee).

# WHEN WERE THE FIRST OLYMPICS?

I don't mind the running;
the javelin's a hoot;

jumping's no problem;
the discus sounds cute;

I'm fine with the boxing;
I'll wrestle a brute;

my chariot's all ready
to begin my pursuit.

There's just one small thing
I'd like to dispute:

do I *really* have to do these
in my birthday suit?

*Poem written by Pantymedes of Thrace on the eve of the first recorded Olympic Games, 776BCE.*

The first recorded Olympic Games were held at Olympia in the Greek city-state of Elis in 776BCE. It is believed, however, that the games had been held for at least 500 years before that. They originally began with foot races, but over time new sports were added, including wrestling, boxing, horse racing, chariot racing and the pentathlon (an event featuring five sports). And yes, in those early Olympics, competitors really did have to take part without any clothes on. If this rule had been insisted on in more recent times, the first modern Olympics (held in Athens in 1896) might have fallen at the first hurdle.

## WHAT ARE RAINBOWS MADE OF?

Whenever I reach out to touch a rainbow,
it disappears into thin air,

and I know deep down it's just a trick,
that it isn't really there,

it's how the sunlight shines through water,
how each colour refracts and bends,

but that doesn't stop me from trying to touch one
or searching for the rainbow's end.

A rainbow is an optical illusion made by sunlight and water droplets. Rainbows form when sunlight shines through water; light reflects off the water droplets in the atmosphere, refracts (bends) and splits into different colours because each colour refracts by different amounts. There is an old Irish legend that there's a pot of gold at the end of a rainbow, guarded by a leprechaun.

## WHY DOES A LION HAVE A MANE?

Is your mane looking worn out and tatty?
Lifeless and lank or lacking in lustre?
Is it fried and frizzled from all of that sun?
Are you losing respect from the lions around you?

Worry no more! Turn the lank into **LUXURIOUS**,
the frizz into **FABULOUS** and the shabby into **SHINE**,
with our new **KING OF THE JUNGLE**
shampoo and conditioner range.

Our **REVOLUTIONARY** pro-vitamin B5 formula
will **SPRUCE** up your mane in no time,
so you can signal to all of your rivals,
this lion is **NOT** to be messed with!

**KING OF THE JUNGLE** uses only the most **NATURAL** ingredients
and is available in a wide range of aromas
from **ROTTING ANTELOPE CARCASS** to **MAXIMUM MUSK** –
all guaranteed to drive your lioness **WILD**!

So come on, **MAINTAIN YOUR MANE**
with **KING OF THE JUNGLE** shampoo and conditioner,
show the youngsters who's **BOSS**
and become the **PRIDE** of your **PRIDE**.

---

The lion is the only cat species that has a mane. By the time a male lion is three years old, his mane is well underway. They can vary a lot in colour and size. The older the lion, though, the darker the mane. It is thought that the lion's mane helps to signal its strength – to impress the lionesses and intimidate other males. And as for being 'King of the Jungle', that might be true if the lion actually lived in one. The lion's nickname comes from a Hindi word which is pronounced similarly to 'jungle' but has a broad definition: a place uninhabited by humans. This includes forests, but also other places such as grasslands and deserts.

# AVAILABLE STYLES

THE 'DANDY'

THE 'COOL CAT'

THE 'MULLET'

THE 'MANE MAN'

THE 'FLAT TOP'

THE 'MID-PARTING'

THE 'HIPPIE'

THE 'BOWL'

KING of the JUNGLE

## WHY DO CLOUDS FLOAT?

Somebody help, I'm under a cloud!
Clouds, I think, should not be allowed
They're not fluffy and fun
Some weigh five hundred tonnes
I get nervous in case they fall down

I'm under a cloud – help me! I said
They fill me with worry – I'm living in dread
They're heavy and scary
They're very precari-
ous – what if one drops on my head?

Yippee! I'm no longer under a cloud!
It's okay, you said. Don't be so cowed –
A cloud is just droplets
So tiny they stop it
From plummeting down to the ground

An average fluffy white cumulus cloud weighs about 500 tonnes: about the same as three adult blue whales. Fortunately, the water or ice particles from which they're formed are too small to feel the effects of gravity. These tiny particles are able to float on the warm air rising up from the ground beneath them. The water droplets condense, sticking together and growing until they eventually become too heavy and fall to the ground as rain. If the air in the cloud is below freezing point, ice crystals form. If the air all the way down to the ground is also freezing, it snows.

## HOW DO ANIMALS SURVIVE IN FREEZING SEAS?

When temperatures dip
and it's as cold as can be

to survive is as easy as . . .
this ABC –

as shown by the herring,
the whale or the ptarmigan,

you need Antifreeze, Blubber or
a (waterproof) Cardigan*

*(but only if it's *feathery and extra, extra, extra, extra thick*)

Fish like the Arctic cod and the Antarctic crocodile icefish have antifreeze in their blood! This is made of natural chemicals that stop them from freezing. Other creatures find ways of insulating themselves: some mammals, such as whales, store fat (blubber). Other mammals, such as sea otters, have fur to keep freezing temperatures at bay. A polar bear has both, grateful for its fur when on snow or ice but relying on its stores of fat when in water.

## ARE BATS THE ONLY FLYING MAMMALS?

My dog is in her workshop again.
She's banging and sawing, clanging and clattering,
measuring and muttering, her drawings
spread out across the bench,
alterations marked in red.

My dog thinks she is getting closer,
claims she actually left the ground on her last attempt,
although I was there, watching
as one of the wheels hit a stone on the path.
Not so much flying as jumping.

She's repaired the wings since,
made a new propeller, readjusted the tail.
There may be a big dent in her crash helmet
but she's tough, she's not giving up.
'It's merely a question of speed,' she says.

And look, here she comes now,
phut-phut-phutting her way down the garden,
being careful to avoid mum's flower beds.
I wave and she gives me a paws-up
through her cockpit window.

'You must be bats if you think you can fly!'
I tell her over the noise of the propeller.
'If only I was!' she shouts back and grins.
She puts on her goggles, takes a deep breath,
and prepares to reach for the sky.

Bats are the only mammals that are able to fly by flapping their wings, although there are other mammals that can glide, such as the flying squirrel, the colugo, the paradise tree snake and the flying frog. It is thought that the ancestors of bats were originally gliders themselves, using that skill to move between trees, but then found that flapping gave them greater control and manoeuvrability.

## DO ELEPHANTS REALLY HOLD EACH OTHER'S TAILS?

Young elephants should be herd and not seen,
and so it was I would walk behind her,
my mum's magnificent bottom a giant grey screen,
as we set off on the long trail for water.

I would hang on to her tail, grip it tightly in my trunk,
knowing that without her, I'd be sunk.
That was many years ago; now my tail is held in turn,
and there are fewer of us on that journey

beneath this Sun, which burns until it dips
below the distant mountains as it slowly sets.
And I think of her, the swish of her tail.
An elephant never forgets.

It's quite common for baby and teenage elephants to hang on to a family member's tail with their trunks when they go on long walks. This guides them and gives them a sense of security. An elephant's tail can grow up to 1.5 metres in length, which means that it hangs down far enough for a calf or a young elephant to grasp the tail firmly in its trunk – as if there weren't enough things for us to love about elephants already.

## WHICH COUNTRY FIRST USED PAPER MONEY?

Money doesn't grow on trees,
or so it's said, but what if
you're from tenth-century China

and you're down the market
sizing up the juicy mangoes and lychees
(which definitely do grow on trees),

maybe some bean sprouts
and a bunch or two of lotus roots,
those peaches looks good, too,

and you reach into your pocket,
only to be reminded that the money
you're holding in your hand

just happens to be made
from the bark of the mulberry tree,
where does that leave you then?

And – on that note –
if money really doesn't grow on trees,
why do banks have branches?

The first known use of paper as some form of currency was by the Chinese during the Tang dynasty (618–907CE), although it was only used by wealthy merchants and government officials. In the Song dynasty (960–1279CE), which followed shortly afterwards, paper money became widespread. The money was printed on dark blue-grey paper made from mulberry bark. So yes, to coin a phrase, money really did grow on trees.

# HOW YOUNG CAN THE US PRESIDENT BE?

I do solemnly swear that I am totally thirty-five years old,
I promise I am, I really am, and not nearly nine and a half,
no matter what Kelly Jenkins says, because she always gets things wrong,
especially in maths as she's too busy talking to Emma Patterson
and never listens to what Miss says,

and I will faithfully execute the Office of President of the United States,
although not on Saturday mornings because that's when
I've got my bassoon lesson and I'm going for my Grade 3,
Mr Olivieri thinks I might get a distinction if I practise more
and improve my concentration a bit, and where was I, oh yes, that's right:

I will – to the best of my ability – preserve, protect and defend
the Constitution of the United States, which should be easy
as I'm really good at judo although it's not on at the moment
because Mrs Newman has put her back out, but I reckon the Constitution
would be pretty safe with me, a lot safer than if Kelly Jenkins was in charge,

Kelly Jenkins couldn't even last two weeks as our class stationery monitor
because she kept flicking rolled up balls of paper with her ruler
and then licked one of the ink pads for a dare, so help me God.

The youngest a US president could possibly be is 35 years old. It's all set out in Article II of the United States Constitution, written way back in 1787. To date, the youngest president has been Theodore Roosevelt: he was 42, which leaves plenty of room for you to try and beat his record. You do also need to have been born in the USA to qualify and have been a resident there for at least 14 years. Oh, and yes, there is also the small matter of winning an election by getting millions and millions of people to vote for you. Other than that, it should be easy.

# WHICH SPORT WAS PLAYED ON THE MOON?

Playing a round of golf upon the Moon
is very much a case
of swings and roundabouts.

On the plus side,
you don't have to putt much effort in
to make the ball travel miles
(which, of course, is a fair, fair way).

On the downside,
there's not much atmosphere
and sooner or later
you lose your golf ball down a crater.

On 6 February 1971, Apollo 14 astronaut Alan Shepard attempted to hit two golf balls on the Moon. While Shepard's own attempts didn't go any great distance, it's been calculated that a professional golfer might be able to hit a ball almost four kilometres on the Moon, given the lack of air resistance and gravity. One small step for a human, maybe, but one giant tee shot for 'golfkind'.

# WHY DO WE GET BRUISES?

My knee has a bruise
with an assortment of hues;
I don't think it knows
which colour to choose.

Three shades of black
and at least seven blues,
it's both purple and red –
it must be confused.

Small wonder my knee
should feel ill at ease,
for blood has oozed forth
from my capillaries.

I tell my knee 'don't worry –
it's the way we repair.'
But my knee takes no notice,
thinks it doesn't seem fair

that the culprit's unbruised
with barely a scuff,
and it glares at the bike
which had made me fall off.

When you bump into something, the tiny blood vessels (capillaries) under your skin break on impact. Blood oozes out of them and collects around where the bump happened with other fluids, because it has nowhere else to go. The red blood cells give the bump a reddish colour. Within hours, the red blood cells start to get reabsorbed back into the body and the bump turns bluish-purple – we call this a bruise. As it starts to fade, the bruise turns greenish or yellowish.

# WHY DOES THE LEANING TOWER OF PISA LEAN?

I laid a margherita down upon weak, uneven ground, and on that laid another, followed by fifty-seven others only to discover my Tower of Pizza had begun to lean and the hopes I'd had for the success of my scheme – or so it would seem – were almost entirely without foundation.

The construction of the Tower of Pisa wasn't even half-complete when it began to lean. The problem was that the foundations of the tower were too shallow. The ground beneath it was also too unstable – Pisa is between two rivers, so it was made of a mixture of clay, sand and shells. Officially completed in 1372, the tower continued to lean further over the next six centuries until work was done to reduce the lean and prevent it from collapsing altogether. The original engineers should have paid more attention to where the placename 'Pisa' came from: it's Greek for 'marshy sands'.

# WHY SHOULD WE RECYCLE?

In an attempt to conserve my energy
and slender natural resources,
this poem has been formed from words
recycled from my previous poems.

These words, in turn, were themselves
recycled from an English dictionary,
which itself was originally forged
from the raw materials of the alphabet.

By recycling and reusing in this manner,
I make sure none of my words go to waste
and I've been able to reduce my carbon wordprint
by more than 50 per cent over the last year.

But I have no plans to stop there.
By 2030, I am looking to phase out words
in my poetry altogether, starting here
with the fifth and final verse of this poem:

                      ,
                               !
       '
                ;
            .

---

Recycling is important as it means materials can be used again and again! This reduces the need to make new materials (such as plastic) and lowers pollution as fewer materials are thrown away. Making new materials also creates a lot of greenhouse gas emissions – gases that contribute to climate change by warming our planet up over time. By recycling, we can help reduce the amount of greenhouse gases being produced. We should think more about what we buy, how it's made, and how recyclable the packaging is – and think twice about whether we need to buy something new in the first place. If we're going to save this planet, we all need to play our part!

## ARE OLYMPIC GOLD MEDALS MADE OF REAL GOLD?

I wish there were gold medals for finishing last –
just think of how many I would have amassed!
I'm hopeless at sport, people say I'm the worst,
when it comes to last place, I always come first.

I'd win a gold medal for the ten-metre crawl,
the short or low jump, or not catching a ball,
knocking down hurdles or the best bellyflop;
at falling off skateboards, I'm sure to come top.

And I know a gold medal is not all it seems –
it's made mainly from silver, yet it still gleams.
But I'm shining, too, because one day you'll see
I'm the best in the world at being me.

Olympic gold medals are 92.5 per cent silver. Only the plating on the outside is gold, and this must be at least six grams of 24 carat pure gold. Silver medals are pure silver, while bronze medals are red brass, which is 95 per cent copper and five per cent zinc. And Olympic medal tables are typically made from oak, maple or mahogany.

## WHAT WAS THE FIRST ANIMAL TO BE CLONED?

Move over, Dolly,
You may have grabbed all the fame
But I'm Tim the Tadpole –
Remember the name!

Because I beat you to it
And yet still I'm unknown.
Yes, I, mighty Tim –
The original clone!

You hit the headlines
Just because you're a sheep.
It would have been me
If I'd made that big leap.

But in the Big Pond of Life,
I was only ever a sprog.
RIP Me,
who was never a frog.

In 1996, Dolly the sheep was cloned using cells from an adult sheep, meaning she was identical to the sheep she was cloned from. She was the first successful mammal clone – but before Dolly came along, there had been a number of other attempts and experiments. In fact, as far back as 1952, tadpoles had been cloned in the USA. However, none of them survived long enough to develop into frogs. Dolly herself lived only six and a half years, approximately half the life expectancy for a sheep. Cloning remains controversial and many people question if it should be done at all; while the process itself is difficult, expensive and dangerous for the animals involved.

# WHO INVENTED THE FIRST CAR?

The answer to that
one might say depenz

on where inventing starts
and inventing enz

for while one person creates,
another amenz

but if pushed, I'd answer
Karl Friedrich Benz.

The problem with inventions is that they are never straightforward. Many people have taken part in the development of the motor car. For instance, back in the early 1500s, artist and inventor Leonardo da Vinci sketched a horseless, mechanised cart. In 1769, Nicolas-Joseph Cugnot built the first self-propelled steam road vehicle; from 1832–1839, Robert Anderson built the first electric carriage; and in 1886, Gottlieb Wilhelm Dailmer and Wilhelm Maybach built an engine that works similarly to car engines today – by burning gasoline (fuel) and turning the heat produced into energy to power the vehicle. Also in 1886, Karl Friedrich Benz created a vehicle with a built-in engine. He was given a patent (a certificate saying that he invented it) for this automobile, along with many other car engineering systems. So yes, he has good reason to go down in history as the inventor, but let's not forget the people who helped him on his way.

# WHO MADE THE FIRST TRIP AROUND THE WORLD?

Following in the footsteps of Ferdinand Magellan,
the fearless Portuguese navigator,
I set off on a voyage of my own,
exploring the white space of the page
in the form of a poem.

The early lines of the poem proceeded without incident.
The vast blankness of the page
no longer appeared so mysterious
as it began to fill with the words I had written upon it,
each one a signpost on my journey.

As my voyage went on, I grew more confident.
I began to explore wider and further, sailing to whole new areas of the page,
charting the hitherto unknown
with metaphors marking the continents of my thoughts,
each simile like an old crumpled map.

Was it when my poem began to ask questions
that I started to lose my bearings? Or had I been blown off course
by storms off the Cape of the Fourth Verse?
It matters little now, for too late it was that I realised
that, unlike Earth, the page was flat

as my words drifted on and on, across the page, beyond its right-hand margin, toppling over the edg

Ferdinand Magellan is often given the credit for being the first person to circumnavigate the world. However, this Portuguese explorer died before he reached home, leaving Spanish Basque navigator Juan Sebastián Elcano to complete the journey in 1522. So Magellan's expedition did circumnavigate the world and, in the process, definitively demonstrated for future generations that the world was round. The journey took about three years – 1,082 days to be exact. Five ships set out, but only one, *Victoria*, returned to Spain in 1522. During their journey, the crews had to cope with difficult weather, diseases, rebellions, and conflicts which often had devastating consequences for local peoples. Magellan and Elcano's expeditions travelled from Spain to South America, across the southern Pacific Ocean to Oceania, then Southeast Asia, across the Indian Ocean to Africa, and along Africa's west coast back up to Spain.

## WHY DO ANIMALS MIGRATE?

I suppose it is a bit of a hike.
We must have done twenty thousand miles, door to door,
not that the Arctic and Antarctic Circles have doors as such,
but you know what I mean.

Why do we do it? Good question.
Well, I'm hardly going out on a wing here
when I say that we Arctic terns just love our sunshine.
It's as simple as that.

All that lovely daylight!
It lights up the ocean, the world around us.
I mean, have you ever tried to find fish or insects in the darkness
of an Arctic winter? I thought not.

Some of the gang were wondering whether
we should go to Cornwall next year.
But personally, I think it gets too busy. Not to mention the prices!
No, it will be the Antarctic again, I hope,

it's a real home from home.
And besides, life is a journey, that's what I think,
and what journey could be more magnificent than ours,
chasing the light, in constant pursuit of the sun.

There can be many reasons behind the seasonal movement of animals from one habitat to another, and back again. Millions journey to find food or water, to seek a mate, or – increasingly so – because of the climate. In Tanzania, there's an event that's called the Great Migration, when more than two million wildebeest journey 800 kilometres across the Serengeti plain in search of food and water. The Arctic tern, though, holds the record for the longest migration, flying from the North Pole to the South Pole and back again. This long trip means they follow the summer sun as it moves around the world.

# WHY DO I NEED TO EAT A LOT OF FRUIT AND VEGETABLES?

Hereby I do solemnly pledge
To eat up all my fruit and veg,
I know such things are good for me –
But spare me from the broccoli.

Spinach, mango, kale, kumquat,
I promise I will eat the lot.
I will even eat a mouldy pea –
If you let me off the broccoli.

Load my plate with Brussels sprouts!
Carrots! Squash! Don't leave them out!
I'll eat them good and properly.
I shall, though, leave my broccoli.

With fruit and veg my body wins
New minerals and vitamins,
But keep one thing from my diet –
Broccoli. Don't make me try it.

It helps to keep the bugs away?
Makes healthy hearts and eyes, you say?
Okay, I sigh, with some regret,
I s'pose I could eat **ONE** floret.

Fruit and vegetables are some of the best sources of vitamins, minerals and fibre that you can find and they should be part of everyone's balanced diet. For example, vegetables such as spinach, and fruit such as mangoes and apricots provide you with vitamin A, which helps your body defend itself against illness and infection. Or, as the saying goes, an apple a day keeps the doctor away – or anybody for that matter, if you throw it hard enough. Not that you should do such a thing, of course.

## WHAT WOOD IS A CRICKET BAT MADE OF?

I don't think there could ever be
a creature more confused than me.
Am I this or am I that?
How strange to be a cricket bat!

Problem is – I can't unpick it –
I share little with the cricket.
I've no antennae. I cannot chirp.
I've tried to jump – it never works.

Yet neither have I batlike things.
I have no fur. I have no wings.
I cannot see by using sound
nor do I sleep upside down.

I'm just some wood, a block of willow,
as useful as an iron pillow,
but then I'm gripped by two gloved hands,
a ball is bowled,

and I understand . . .

Cricket bats can be made from different woods, but the most common ones are English white willow and Kashmir willow. Bats are treated with raw (unboiled) linseed oil to toughen the hitting surface and reduce the chances of them cracking or splitting. This is not much of an issue whenever I'm batting as it's very rare that my bat ever makes contact with the ball.

# WHICH ANIMAL HIDES THE BEST?

**CHAMELEON**
Who's the best? Guilty as charged!
I'm the true master of camouflage,
I can change the colour of my skin –
sometimes chameleons just wanna blend in.

**ARCTIC HARE**
They seek her here, they seek her there,
The mysterious, elusive Arctic hare.
It's as if she just vanished into thin air –
First she was here, now she's snowhere.

## MIMIC OCTOPUS

And the winner of the Animal Impersonator of the Year award
With his impression of a poisonous flatfish
Goes to . . .
The mimic octopus
With a score of eight out of ten . . . tacles

## CRAB SPIDER

Has anybody spied a crab spider?
Three-time Olympic champion hider.
She headed off to sniff some flowers.
I've not seen her now for seven hours.

## STICK INSECT

to hide in a forest,

try this trick,

turn yourself into a stick

There are quite a few contenders for the animal that hides the best – and I wouldn't like to pick a winner. I probably wouldn't be able to spot them in the first place, to be honest. But the chameleon is rightly famous for its ability to change colour and pattern. In a layer below its transparent skin, it has cells called chromatophores that react to sunlight, heat and emotion, by changing colour. And the mimic octopus can not only change its colour but do very good impersonations of the banded sea snake and some fish.

As water drips through the ceiling of a cave, it leaves behind tiny traces of calcium carbonate and other minerals. Over thousands of years, these minerals form into icicle-shaped rocks – stalactites (with a 'c' for ceiling). Below them, on the ground where the water droplets land, minerals also build up, forming mounds of rock called stalagmites (with a 'g' for ground). Given the words are so similar, it can be very easy to get them muddled up; that's why I always carry a dictionary with me whenever I am walking through a cave.

# WHAT ARE ANIMALS WITHOUT A BACKBONE CALLED?

Some call them adderspears and attercops, drumble-drones and squirm-in-the grounds, bibblebugs and slugabeds, chiselhogs and hopalots, fuzzypigs and shufflepinchers, flutterbies and shuckalongs, flibberflobbers and bobbydazzlers, or nightcrawlers and scuttleshells, sting-lanterns and glowcumbers, sidlepinchers and nip-me-quicklies, inksquirters and gutterpeelers, billywitches and barnabees, blobberlobs and dawdledailies, ticklelegs and johnny-come-slowlies, slouchpickles and legclingers, suckerpods and squidges, pricklebushes and bustle-me-ways.

Or, if you're short on time, you can just call them invertebrates.

More than 95 per cent of all known living animal species are invertebrates – creatures that do not have a backbone or an internal bony skeleton. Some are soft-bodied, such as jellyfish, worms and slugs; others, such as beetles, spiders and crabs, have a hard outer casing called an exoskeleton. The largest group of invertebrates are insects; scientists think there could be up to 10 million different species. For ants alone, there are an estimated 20 quadrillion of them. That's 20,000,000,000,000,000!

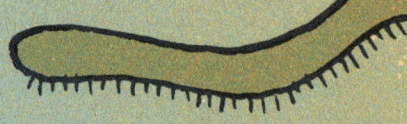

# WHAT IS A DIMENSION?

At the length of his fame,
Tom thought he knew so much about dimensions
that he would talk about them
at great width.

Tom's knowledge, however,
was often high of the mark,
and he'd always run out of the fourth one
before he'd even got to it.

In mathematics, a dimension is a measurement of space: the first dimension (1-D) is length; the second (2-D), is length and width; and the third (3-D) is length, width and height. The world around us has three dimensions, whereas a line has just one and the surface of something has two. According to physicists, there's a fourth dimension, too, which is time. Combined with the other three dimensions, it shows the position of an event in time and space. Pretty deep, eh?

## WAS BLACKBEARD A REAL PIRATE?

Foul, scurvy knave, are you questioning me?
For I be as real as the deepest blue sea!
Come, let us parley – bring thy whole motley crew
& I'll teach you dumb dogs a sharp thing or two.

Because that be my name – young Edward Teach –
With two swords & one pistol within easy reach,
& a knife hid beneath my large tricorn hat
& my world-famous beard, long, thick and black,

in which, weaved with hemp, I might then light a match
to terrify the britches off some poor bilge rat
& oh, how I'd laugh as he'd cry out for help –
Come quick! he would shout. It's the devil himself!

& the rest of the crew would beg, Heavens forfend!
while we in the good ship, the Queen Anne's Revenge
would seize all their cargo, their treasure & goods.
What can I say? It was my livelihood

& all of us need to find a way to get by.
Buccaneering was mine – do ye savvy? Aye, aye!
'Til that fateful last day, when came my final avast.
Dead men tell no tales? I say, scupper that.

Yes, he absolutely was. Edward Teach (c.1680–1718) is one of the most famous of all the pirates, going about his buccaneering business in the Caribbean Sea and Atlantic Ocean. However, he wasn't a particularly successful pirate and his career lasted only about 15 months before he was cornered by soldiers and sailors in North Carolina and reportedly shot five times and stabbed more than 20. He was a rather fearsome individual, though. During battle, he would sometimes weave strings into his beard which he would light. The smoke they gave off would give him an intimidating appearance

# DO CATS ALWAYS LAND ON THEIR FEET?

A CAT FALLING, ASLEEP

Sorry, did you say something?
I was busy dreaming about a mouse.
I spend most of the day asleep, you know –
you see, I really love this house

with its choice of comfy chairs
or, if I fancy it, a lap
and a real log fire to warm myself . . .
. . .
. . .
soz, just had another nap.

Where was I? Ah yes, this place!
I feel quite at home, it must be said.
There's a family of humans who report to me –
I get pampered, stroked and fed

and sometimes . . . . . . . . . . . . .
. . . . . .
. . . . .
Oh no, did I nod off again?
I must have had too many treats.
Anyway, you were saying something –
about me landing on my feet?

The cat in this poem has the most wonderful lazy life of luxury – so in that sense, it has 'landed on its feet'. But when cats fall, do they always literally land on their feet? Their safety depends on the height of the fall – but it must be said that cats are rather brilliant at falling. The cat's pyjamas, in fact. They have an unconscious ability to orient themselves when falling – called the 'righting reflex' – as well as an amazing sense of balance and a very flexible backbone for turning quickly. Indeed, it's thought that cats can fall two storeys of a building and still walk (or hobble) away with no more than minor injuries.

# ARE HORSES EVEN- OR ODD-TOED?

writing poems
on the hoof

can be quite hard
to tell the troof

the tricky theme
of horses' toes

is harder than
one might suppose

but nothing helps more
than this fact will:

the horse, you see, is
perissodactyl

but does it have
one toe or five?

science, it seems
cannot decide

the only cert's
that they're odd-toed

hereby endeth
this odd ode

Horses have an odd number of toes, like other animals such as donkeys, zebras, tapirs and rhinos. These odd-toed animals are called perissodactyls. The horse's hoof itself is really an enlarged toe. Studies examining how the horse has evolved over millions of years suggest that the ridges on modern horse hooves were once distinct toes – and so horses may have had five toes after all. That's the thing about modern science: its findings really do keep you on your toes.

## ARE COAL AND DIAMONDS THE SAME THING?

Not a diamond.
I give you this lump of coal.
It is a broken chunk of starless night.
It will not sparkle on your finger.

Take it.
For this rock is made of carbon, too.
Its atoms may be less compressed
and it may not be as pure,
but it will offer warmth when you need it.

Three hundred million years,
this lump of coal's been waiting
to have you hold it
in your hand.

I am too poor for diamonds.
I hope you understand.

Coal and diamonds are both made of an element called carbon, but they are created in different ways, leading to differences in structure and appearance. Coal is formed when rotting leaves, seeds and dead wood get pressed down in the ground over millions of years. Because of the mixture of materials, the carbon in coal is mixed with other elements such as nitrogen and sulfur. Diamonds, on the other hand, are made from carbon found deep under Earth's surface at high temperatures and pressure. These conditions transform the carbon into a transparent, extremely hard material.

# WHAT IS THE JET STREAM?

**WHOOSH!** . . . I'm sorry but it's really no use, I think I'll have to tell you later – my words, it seems, are in a jet stream where the currents are much greater . . .

Sorry about that. I'm just catching my breath. Right then . . . jet streams are bands of strong wind that usually blow from east to west across Earth. They occur when warm air masses meet cold air masses in the atmosphere, eight to 14 kilometres above Earth's surface. A jet stream can push a plane close to the speed of sound. Increased winds in the jet stream have seen flight times from New York to London reduce, sometimes by as much as nearly an hour.

## WHAT IS ABSOLUTE ZERO?

Ladies and gentlemen, please put your hands together
and give the coldest of cold welcomes
to the temperature on everybody's frozen lips,
that Magnificent Muffler of Molecular Motion,
the Expert Expeller of Effervescence and Energy
and Numinous Number of Nullified Numbness,
the Crowned Conqueror and Commander-in-Chief
of The Out-and-Out Nought, The Great Big Nil,
and The Complete and Utter Zilch,
yes, I'm talking about the Coldest and the Boldest,
the Chilliest and the Thrilliest,
the Freeziest, the Beezkneeziest,
the Temperature Far from Easiest,
the very lowest of the low
it's the one and only . . . **ABSOLUTE ZERO!**

Absolute zero is the coldest temperature that scientists believe is possible: −273.15°C. It is sometimes measured using the Kelvin scale as 0°K, named after a scientist who researched these low temperatures. The closest scientists have got to creating this temperature is Very Nearly Absolute Zero in 2021, when scientists in Bremen, Germany, cooled some rubidium atoms (a type of metal) to 38 trillionths of a degree above 0°K.

## CAN IT RAIN FISH?

And now for today's weather forecast.
After a bright start, a tornado will blow in
from the east, bringing with it winds

of up to seventy miles an hour,
followed by the possibility of showers of fish
across some coastal areas.

Further inland, a deluge of frogs is likely,
while those in the south may see
flurries of worms, crabs and snakes

with the occasional outbreak of jellyfish.
For those of you in the north,
a Falling Spider Warning has been issued

and you're advised to hide in a cupboard all day.
Finally, reports are coming in of an alligator
lifted up into the sky by a waterspout

so you might want to wrap up warm
and wear a helmet. Tomorrow's outlook:
variable with a chance of toads.

Yes, it can 'rain' fish – and all sorts of other creatures, too. It can happen when a tornado or waterspout sucks up the animals; then they are blown around inside the spinning wind until the wind speed decreases and the creatures fall down. In Yoro, Honduras, it has rained fish every year for around 100 years. It's not just fish, though. Elsewhere in the world, animals that have 'rained' include snakes, spiders, worms – and even alligators and cattle. In 2012 in Kentucky, USA, one family found their horse in the kitchen! A tornado had lifted off their roof and lifted the horse from the stable and into the house. Amazingly, the horse survived.

# HOW LONG IS THE MARATHON?

Training for a race
of twenty-six point two miles
might not sound like much fun,

but you'll find it's worth it,
in the long run.

These days, the distance for a marathon is 42.1 kilometres (26.2 miles), but it hasn't always been that. In fact, in 490 BCE when the Athenian messenger Pheidippides ran from the site of the battle of Marathon to Athens with the message 'Victory', it was quite a bit longer: 240 kilometres. It took him two days. When the modern Olympics began in Athens, Greece, in 1896, it was roughly 40 kilometres, but that was amended for the 1908 London Olympics. The race was due to start at Windsor Castle and finish in the White City Stadium (a distance of 42 kilometres) but the King wanted the runners to start the race from where it could be seen by the royal children in their nursery. The runners had to go a bit further, and it's been the same length ever since!

# HOW DID PEOPLE MAKE THE FIRST TOOLS IF THEY DID NOT HAVE TOOLS?

me Stone Age Tony
on today episode of Make Cave Nice
me show how make tool
when have no tool

first, find stone
must be right kind of stone*
hard but can make shape
whack with big rock if not sure

carry on hit with rock (or bone or antler)
'til stone right shape
then strike edge of stone 'til sharp
you now have tool

use tool to make axe
or clean animal skin
or carve wood
or as part of attractive set of cutlery for dinner party

that all from Stone Age Tony
on next episode of Make Cave Nice
me show how make lovely coffee table
out of stone
and bones of enemy

*flint good, shale bad*

Early humans were good at knapping. By that, I don't mean sleeping but the process by which a stone can be shaped and sharpened using a rock or another hard object, such as a piece of antler or bone. This technique was used to make tools. It was important to find the right kind of stone for the job, though – flint, quartzite, chert, basalt and obsidian are all good materials as they flake when struck, rather than splinter. And while all this might sound rather primitive, much skill is involved: do not knock the knack of knapping.

# WHY DO SOME ANIMALS HAVE POUCHES?

I wasn't born yesterday, you know.
Actually, I was. That's why I'm here,
inside this soft and furry padded pouch,
lacking sight and feet and hair.

I'm more jellybean than joey, to be honest with you.

For the next eight months, this will be my home.
My last place, don't mean to knock it
but four weeks in, I had to pack my bags
then crawl and climb into this pocket.

Although it was nice to get a little bit of fresh air.

Elephants get nearly two years to grow inside
before they emerge. Given that, what do you expect?
Barely have they blinked in the light
before they're taking their first steps.

They do still look ever so funny and clumsy, though.

As for me – a baby kangaroo! –
for now, I have to put all that on hold.
Until the time comes, I'll be in this pouch
while developments unfold.

I am confident, however, that one day I can make that jump.

Animals that have pouches in which to raise and carry their young are called marsupials. Species include kangaroos, sugar gliders, koalas, wombats, wallabies and quolls. Their babies need the protection of the pouch, called a marsupium, in which to grow until they are developed enough to leave; the pouches contain teats on which they suckle milk. The babies are very undeveloped when born because of a marsupial's very short gestation period (how long the mother is pregnant). A kangaroo's pregnancy, for instance, lasts a mere four weeks. At the other end of the scale, elephants are pregnant for about 22 months (almost two years), the longest gestation period of all mammals.

## WHICH COUNTRY HAS THE MOST BICYCLES?

My bicycle has been dreaming about the Netherlands.
He would like to go there one day.
They know how to treat a bicycle over there, he tells me.
Dedicated cycle paths: wide ones, too.
And the parking! You can take your pick of spaces, he says.

I don't know where he gets this information,
given that he's a bicycle and therefore cannot read.
He rarely watches travel programmes. I believe him, though.
He says that for the Dutch, the bike is always right;
on their roads, it's the cars who have to mind their manners.

I can hear the pedals of his mind turning over.
There is a distinct absence of hills, he continues.
Yes, a very flat country, by all accounts.
One where a bicycle is not so much a bicycle
but a trusted friend and companion upon the journey of life.

Okay! Okay! I say. I'll look into it.
He flashes his front light three times in approval.

In terms of actual numbers of bicycles, it's no surprise that China has the most: approximately 450 million. But when you look at which country has the most cyclists as a percentage of its population, it's the Netherlands with a whopping 99 per cent. Bikes really are a way of life there, with around 18 million inhabitants owning around 24 million bikes. It must help that the terrain is so flat, but far more than that, the country has built up a vast network of cycle paths, making the bicycle the easiest, cheapest and greenest way to get around.

# HOW MANY DIMPLES ARE THERE ON A GOLF BALL?

My best feature? Mmm . . . that's hard!

Some might say it's my figure – my sphere –
which may not be perfect
but allows me to spin through space
like a tiny, whirling, planet.

Others might point to something inside of me,
the solid softness of my core,
and all the energy it gives to me
to help keep me moving forward.

But I guess – for me – it's got to be my dimples.
After all, everyone loves a dimple!
Three hundred and fifty miniature craters
proudly pockmarking my surface,

and conjuring up that thin layer of air
to send me further on my journey.
I'm telling you, I would not have got to
where I am today without them.

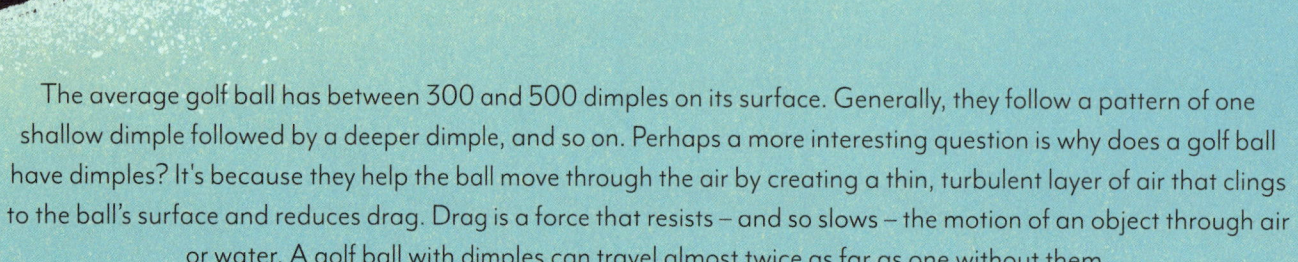

The average golf ball has between 300 and 500 dimples on its surface. Generally, they follow a pattern of one shallow dimple followed by a deeper dimple, and so on. Perhaps a more interesting question is why does a golf ball have dimples? It's because they help the ball move through the air by creating a thin, turbulent layer of air that clings to the ball's surface and reduces drag. Drag is a force that resists – and so slows – the motion of an object through air or water. A golf ball with dimples can travel almost twice as far as one without them.

## WHICH MOUNTAIN IS THE HIGHEST IN THE WORLD?

I didn't climb Mount Everest today.
I went to school.

For the first time since coming here,
I joined in with football
in the playground at lunchtime.

I made a joke during maths
and my classmates all laughed.

At home time, a girl smiled at me
and said see you tomorrow.

I didn't climb Mount Everest today.
I went to school.
So why do I feel twenty-nine thousand feet tall?
Why do I feel like I'm on top of the world?

Mount Everest, on the Tibet-Nepal border, is generally regarded as the highest mountain in the world, at 8,848 metres above sea level. In 1953, Edmund Hillary, a New Zealand mountaineer, and Tenzing Norgay, a Nepali-Indian Sherpa mountaineer, became the first confirmed people to reach its peak. (The Sherpa are a people who live in the mountains around the area of Mount Everest.) Everest might be the highest mountain, but here are some other honourable mentions: the summit of Mount Chimborazo in the Andes mountains in Ecuador, South America, is the furthest point from Earth's centre at 6,310 metres; and Mauna Kea on the island of Hawaii, USA, is the tallest mountain when measured from base to peak at 10,205 metres. More than half of Mauna Kea, however, is under the sea.

# WHICH RIVER IS THE LONGEST?

'Do we really have to make everything a competition?' sighed the Yangtze. 'Why can't we just go with the flow?'

'I agree,' murmured the Volga. 'It's simply too vulgar.'

'And besides, why does it have to be the longest?' said the Congo. 'Surely, what's more important is depth.'

'You would say that. You're 220 metres deep in places!' said the Yenisei. 'Although I do feature the world's deepest lake,' it added, meandering off in a whole new direction.

'Perhaps, we should have a race instead. You know, see who's the fastest.' That was the Mississippi, who thought itself zippy.

'Yes, a race could be fun,' agreed the Amazon. 'After all, rivers do run.'

'But you'd win it easy!' gushed the Zambezi. 'You're the fastest. And the widest.'

'I'm the longest, too,' the Amazon answered, considering itself to be at its prime.

'I wouldn't bank on it,' said the Indus. 'I think you need to check your sources.'

A flood of arguments and counter-arguments followed until one voice raised itself above the babble in an attempt to build a bridge over the troubled waters.

'Look, the problem is that you're in denial,' said the Nile. 'We all know the answer to this question is me. But none of that matters. What's important is the water that flows in our channels, whilst we weave through this planet, carving out landscapes, connecting all life.'

The rivers fell still in silent reflection. After a while, the first ripples returned and they resumed their business.

The Nile is indeed credited with being the longest river in the world, with a length of 6,695 kilometres. It starts around the Equator (the imaginary line running around the middle of Earth) in East Africa and flows north before finally reaching the Nile Delta in Egypt, where it flows out into the Mediterranean Sea. There are counter-claims that the Amazon might be the longest, but that depends on where you believe it starts. If its actual source begins with the Apurímac River, the Amazon river system would be slightly longer than the Nile – but this is disputed. The Amazon, however, is the undisputed champ of volume – it discharges more freshwater into the ocean than the next seven largest rivers combined.

## CAN YOU SAY THE ALPHABET IN CODE?

My alternative phonetic alphabet
**A** is for aisle – no, that doesn't quite work
**B** is for bee – this is going to drive me berserk
**C** is for sea – hang on, that's not right at all
**D** is for double-u – now I feel like a fool
**E** is for eye – a choice better unseen
**F** is for four – four fours are sixteen
**G** is for gnat – although it sounds like it's gnot
**H** is for heir – is that really all that I've got?
**I** is for one – if you're from ancient Rome
**J** is for jalapeño – best not said but shown
**K** is for know – yes, I know that's all wrong
**L** is for Llanfairpwllgwyngyllgogerychwyrndrobwllllantysiliogogogoch – which is a little too long

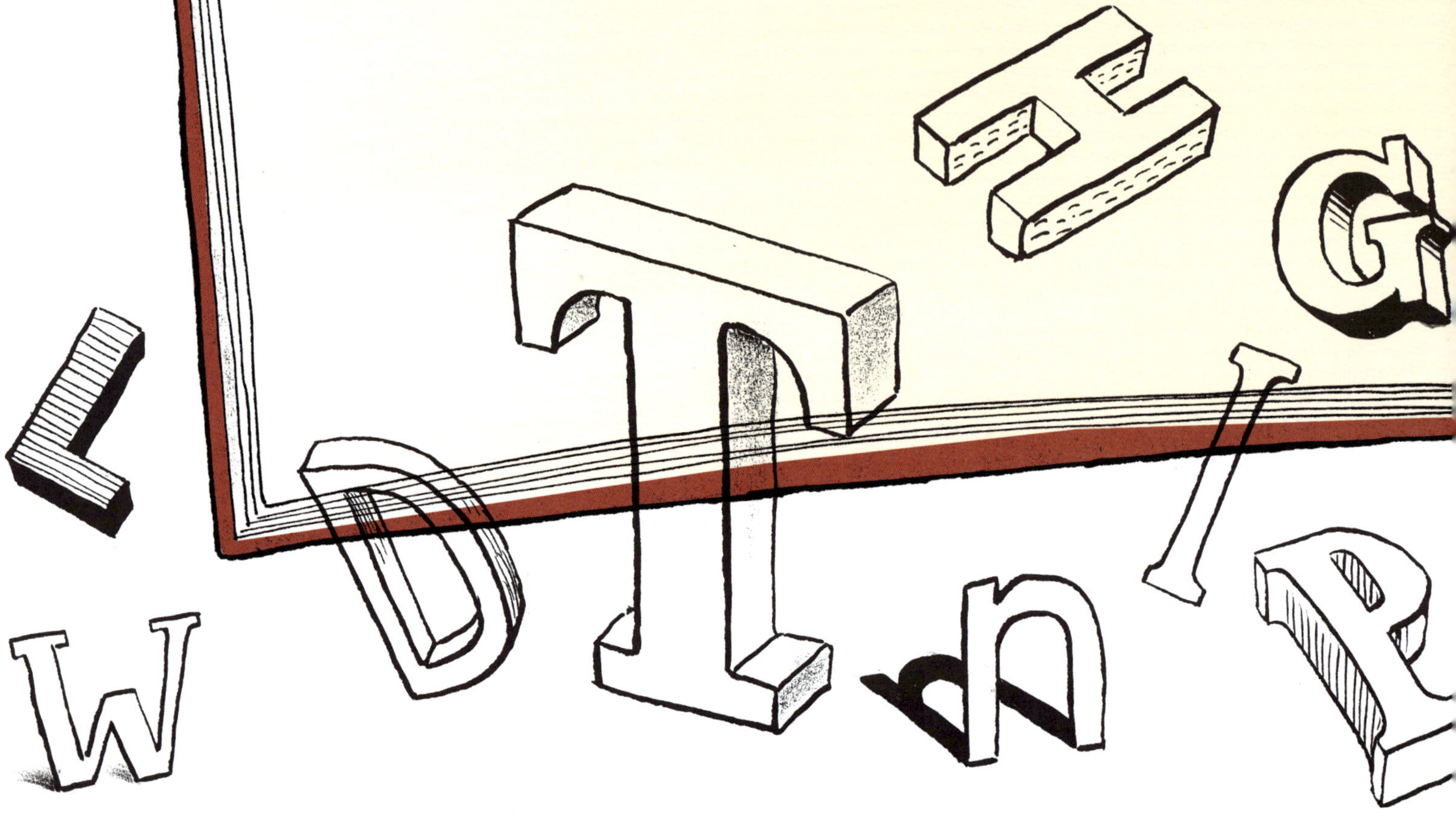

M is for mnemonic – although please don't remind me
N is for entrance – I need to put this behind me
O is for zero – oh, this whole thing's absurd!
P is for pterodactyl – an unhelpful word
Q is for queue – those vowels could give it a miss
R is for are you still reading this?
S is for sea – although it sounds like it isn't
T is for tsunami – which is hardly sufficient
U is for umm . . . I think I might cry
V is for five – that's the same joke as I
W is for why – best to leave that unsaid
X is for xylophone – although it sounds like a zed
Y is for you – whom I feel sorry for
Z is for zzzzzz – it seems you've started to snore

Coding systems for the alphabet have been developed over the years as a way to make communication clearer. The most commonly used one is the NATO Phonetic alphabet, which was devised to allow messages to be exchanged accurately between armed forces of the different NATO member countries. Here it is: Alfa, Bravo, Charlie, Delta, Echo, Foxtrot, Golf, Hotel, India, Juliett, Kilo, Lima, Mike, November, Oscar, Papa, Quebec, Romeo, Sierra, Tango, Uniform, Victor, Whiskey, X-ray, Yankee, Zulu. Other coding systems are available, for example, Morse Code, a system for sending coded messages using combinations of dots and dashes (or, as it's known in Morse Code [...]: -- --- .- .... / -.-. --- -..).

## WHO IS THE CHAMPION WEIGHTLIFTER OF THE ANIMAL WORLD?

You join us at what is set to be a very exciting final day
of this year's extraordinary world championships,
in which we have Hercules Hornwaggler,
the rhinoceros beetle from northern Venezuela,
up against Bill 'Biceps' Bradshaw,
a human fitness instructor from Stourbridge, England,
as they both compete to be crowned
the Champion Weightlifter of the World.

It will be interesting to see whether yesterday's
gruelling semi-final with Alejandra Lopez,
the wily leafcutter ant from Mexico,
will have taken its toll on young Hornwaggler.
Bradshaw, of course, comes into the final fresh,
having awarded himself a bye through
each of the previous rounds, on the grounds
that human beings 'are the best at everything'.

INVITE ME ROUND TO PAGE 10/11

And so here comes Hornwaggler –
I don't believe it . . . he's going for the tree bark!
What a move from the mercurial minibeast!
Look at those magnificent horns sweeping into action,
lifting, lifting – and . . . he's done it!
It's there, above his head! The judges arriving
to measure now . . . and it's 850 times his own weight!
Remarkable – a new world record!

Remember, Bradshaw has to lift the equivalent
in order to stay in this contest. If he doesn't,
the trophy is Hornwaggler's. The arena's all set up:
twenty motor cars for Bradshaw to hoist
in one go . . . he'll be out in the arena very soon . . .
any minute now. Not quite sure what the delay is.
What? He's disappeared? Bradshaw?! **BRADSHAW?!**
I say, has anyone here seen Bradshaw?

Yes, the rhinoceros beetle is the Champion Weightlifter of the World, capable of lifting 850 times its own weight with its horns. The human equivalent would be lifting 55 tonnes. As for mammals, maximum respect to the gorilla, who can lift up to 2,000 kilograms (10 times its own weight!), and the tiger, who can carry prey almost twice its bodyweight. All of this makes me think what an amazing spectacle an Animal Olympics would be, although I appreciate that it might be difficult to organise some of the competitors (and the 'slow race' between a sloth and a snail might get a little boring).

# GLOSSARY

**Air resistance** – A force created by friction, slowing down objects travelling through the air.

**Amulet** – An object thought to give good luck to its owner.

**Antenna** – A long, thin feeler attached to an insect's head.

**Aqueduct** – A bridge designed to carry water.

**Atoms** – Extremely tiny particles that make up the Universe.

**Atrium** – The upper part of the left and right side of the heart.

**Buoyancy** – An object's ability to float in liquid or in the air.

**Canopic jars** – Storage containers for human organs, used by ancient Egyptians in mummification.

**Cell** – A small unit or building block that makes up living things such as plants or animals.

**Clone** – An organism created in a laboratory, identical to the organism it was made from.

**Colossus** – A very large statue.

**Compound** – Something that is made from more than one element (such as carbon dioxide, made from carbon and oxygen).

**Condensation** – Droplets that form when hot water vapour touches a cold surface.

**Cretaceous** – A period of the Mesozoic era from 145–66 million years ago, when many dinosaurs walked Earth.

**Crust** – The outer layer of Earth.

**Cumulus** – A type of cloud with a fluffy appearance.

**Dehydration** – When the body doesn't have enough water to function properly.

**Element** – An element is a substance made from only one type of atom e.g. oxygen.

**Evaporation** – The process through which a liquid becomes a gas.

**Excrement** – Another word for poo.

**Extinct** – (Of a species) having no living members.

**Faeces** – Another word for poo.

**Femur** – The thigh bone.

**Fibula** – A bone in the lower part of the leg.

**Friction** – A force between two objects sliding against one another.

**Galaxy** – A large group of stars and planets. Earth's galaxy is called the Milky Way.

**Genus** – A group of animals that make up a bigger family. For example, *panthera* is a genus of the felidae (cat) family that includes lions and tigers.

**Humerus** – A bone in the upper arm.

**Jurassic** – A period of the Mezosoic era that came before the Cretaceous period, 201–145 million years ago.

**Kelvin scale** – A scale used around the world for measuring temperature.

**Keratin** – A material found in nails and animal hooves.

**Mantle** – The layer between Earth's crust and core.

**Mausoleum** – A building made to hold graves.

**Metacarpal** – A bone in the hand connecting the wrists to the thumb and finger bones.

**Metatarsal** – A bone in the foot connecting the ankles to the toes.

**Methane** – A colourless gas with no smell. It is one of the gases present in farts!

**Minerals** – Chemical elements that our bodies need to develop healthily.

**Mitosis** – The process through which living cells divide into multiple cells.

**Mnemonic** – A rhyme or pattern of letters that helps trigger memory.

**Molecule** – Two or more atoms bonded together.

**NATO** – North Atlantic Treaty Organisation; a group of countries, including France, the UK and Canada, that agree to defend each other against attack.

**Optical illusion** – When the brain perceives an image in a way that doesn't match what it actually looks like.

**Papyri** – A collection of documents made of papyrus, a material used in ancient Egypt.

**Pentathlon** – A sporting competition made up of five different events.

**Phonetic alphabet** – A set of words used in place of letters of the alphabet, to make spelling aloud easier.

**Red blood cells** – A type of blood cell that carries oxygen around the body.

**Reflect** – (Of light) to bounce off a surface.

**Refract** – (Of light) to bend at a particular point, such as when going into water.

**Satellite** – An object that travels around a large body in space, such as a planet.

**Scapula** – The bone of the shoulder blade.

**Sternum** – The flat bone at the front of the chest.

**Tibia** – A bone in the lower part of the leg.

**Ventricle** – A chamber in the lower part of the heart.

**Vortex** – A spinning mass of water or air that can pull objects into it.

**Waterspout** – A tornado that happens on water.

**Woodworm** – A beetle larva that eats wood.

## ABOUT THE AUTHOR

**BRIAN BILSTON** has written poetry collections on pets, football, Christmas and much more. His poems are full of humour, heart and energy, and with over 500,000 followers on social media, he has become truly loved by the online community.

## ABOUT THE ILLUSTRATOR

**JOE BERGER** is a Bristol-based illustrator, animator and cartoonist. Joe has illustrated over 40 children's books including Frank Cottrell-Boyce's *Chitty Chitty Bang Bang* books. He is a past official illustrator for World Book Day and winner of Booktrust's Best New Illustrators Award.